E DUE

GOD IN PROCESS THOUGHT

STUDIES IN PHILOSOPHY AND RELIGION

1. FREUND, E.R. *Franz Rosenzweig's Philosophy of Existence: An Analysis of* The Star of Redemption. 1979. ISBN 90 247 2091 5.

2. OLSON, A.M. *Transcendence and Hermeneutics: An Interpretation of the Philosophy of Karl Jaspers.* 1979. ISBN 90 247 2092 3.

3. VERDU, A. *The Philosophy of Buddhism.* 1981. ISBN 90 247 2224 1.

4. OLIVER, H.H. *A Relational Metaphysic.* 1981. ISBN 90 247 2457 0.

5. ARAPURA, J.G. *Gnosis and the Question of Thought in Vedānta.* 1985. ISBN 90 247 3061 9.

6. HOROSZ, W. and CLEMENTS, T. *Religion and Human Purpose.* 1985. ISBN 90 247 3000 7.

7. SIA, S. *God in Process Thought.* 1985. ISBN 90 247 3103 8.

GOD IN PROCESS THOUGHT

A Study in Charles Hartshorne's Concept of God

SANTIAGO SIA

with a postscript by
CHARLES HARTSHORNE

1985 **MARTINUS NIJHOFF PUBLISHERS**
a member of the KLUWER ACADEMIC PUBLISHERS GROUP
DORDRECHT / BOSTON / LANCASTER

Distributors

for the United States and Canada: Kluwer Academic Publishers, 190 Old Derby Street, Hingham, MA 02043, USA
for the UK and Ireland: Kluwer Academic Publishers, MTP Press Limited, Falcon House, Queen Square, Lancaster LA1 1RN, UK
for all other countries: Kluwer Academic Publishers Group, Distribution Center, P.O. Box 322, 3300 AH Dordrecht, The Netherlands

Library of Congress Cataloging in Publication Data

```
Sia, Santiago.
  God in process thought.

  (Studies in philosophy and religion ; v. 7)
  Bibliography: p.
  1. Hartshorne, Charles, 1897-    --Theology.
2. God--History of doctrines--20th century.  I. Title.
II. Series: Studies in philosophy and religion
(Martinus Nijhoff Publishers) ; v. 7.
B945.H354S5  1985        211        84-22686
ISBN 90-247-3103-8
```

3 7 3 3 2

SEP 10 1985

ISBN 90-247-3103-8

PRINTED IN THE NETHERLANDS

DEDICATION

To my wife,
MARIAN

a source of joy,
a reason for hope,
and
a constant inspiration

TABLE OF CONTENTS

LIST OF ABBREVIATIONS

Reference to Hartshorne's books will be made by means of an abbreviation (see below) followed by page numbers. His articles and other writings will be cited by their full titles and page references. Details regarding these publications are given in the bibliography.

PPS   – *The Philosophy and Psychology of Sensation*, 1934

BH   – *Beyond Humanism: Essays in the New Philosophy of Nature*, 1937

MV   – *Man's Vision of God and the Logic of Theism*, 1941

DR   – *The Divine Relativity: a Social Conception of God*, 1948

WMW – *Whitehead and the Modern World: Science, Metaphysics, and Civilization, Three Essays on the Thought of Alfred North Whitehead*, 1950

RSP   – *Reality as Social Process: Studies in Metaphysics and Religion*, 1953

PSG   – *Philosophers Speak of God*, 1953

LP   – *The Logic of Perfection and Other Essays in Neoclassical Metaphysics*, 1962

AD   – *Anselm's Discovery*, 1967

NTOT – *A Natural Theology for Our Time*, 1967

CSPM – *Creative Synthesis and Philosophic Method*, 1970

WP   – *Whitehead's Philosophy: Selected Essays, 1935 – 1970*, 1972

AW   – *Aquinas to Whitehead: Seven Centuries of Metaphysics of Religion*, 1976

WVR   – *Whitehead's View of Reality*, 1981

IOGT – *Insights and Oversights of Great Thinkers: an Evaluation of Western Philosophy*, 1983

OOTM– *Omnipotence and Other Theological Mistakes*, 1984

CAP   – *Creativity in American Philosophy*, 1984

INTRODUCTION

One of the controversial issues which have recently come into prominence among philosophers and theologians is how one should understand the term God.[1] It seems that, despite the fact that a certain idea of God is assumed by many, if not most, people, there is a degree of disagreement over the meaning of the term. "God" is generally taken to refer to a supreme Being, the Creator, who is perfect and self-existent, holy, personal and loving. This understanding of "God" corresponds to what many have either been brought up to believe in or have come to accept as *the* meaning of this word. Nevertheless, theists appear to be defending a particular idea of God and to be accusing atheists of attacking another, one which does not tie in with the theistic interpretation. Cardinal Maximos IV, for instance, is quoted as saying, "The God the atheists don't believe in is a God I don't believe in either."[2] On the other hand, atheists have been challenging believers to explain clearly what they mean by "God" because these critics cannot see how that idea can have any acceptable meaning. Furthermore, theists themselves seem to be divided over the issue. H.P. Owen in his book *Concepts of Deity* shows quite convincingly that there is "a bewildering variety of concepts of God" among theists.[3] One has only to ask around for confirmation of this observation.

This shift in emphasis from debating whether or not God exists to evaluating the meaningfulness of the term God is probably due to the influence of linguistic analysis, which insists that the words we use ought to be clarified. In fact, it has been argued that the task of clarifying what is meant by "God" must be undertaken first before we can set about the apparently fruitless work of proving whether there is a God or not.[4] Moreover, irrespective of the question of God's existence, the fact that people continue to use and have some basic understanding of this term means that there is need to probe further into the logical sense of "God".

Another possible reason for this state of affairs is that many are becoming aware of a discrepancy between our basic experience of God and the conceptualization of that experience. Obviously, in articulating a fundamental intuition or direct experience, one always runs the risk of failing to do full justice to it. Hence, sometimes what results at the conceptual stage is quite different from what took place at the experiential level. When this happens, there can be a conflict between experience and conceptuality. Pascal had felt this when he remarked that the God of the philosophers was not the God of Abraham, Isaac and Jacob. For Pascal there was a marked contrast between the philosophers' concept and the believers' concrete experience of God. There is an increasing number of people who claim that traditional attempts to formulate what we believe God to be do not lead to a concept which matches our basic beliefs, and is therefore inadequate.

A contemporary thinker who has spent considerable time exploring the God-problem is Charles Hartshorne.[5] He has attempted to provide a philosophical framework with which one can logically, consistently and adequately understand what religiously is meant by "God". Hartshorne is an original thinker who, in a number of books and articles, has set out and elaborated a concept of God which has recently been referred to as a process concept of God and which has become very influential in philosophy of religion and in theology. He has persistently maintained that the classical view of God as absolute, perfect, infinite and immutable is an incorrect translation into philosophical categories of a central religious insight. Accordingly, he is proposing an alternative way of rendering intelligible what religion means by "God".

Hartshorne's efforts may be compared with those of the early Christian Jews who sought the help of philosophy in expressing their religious beliefs. These Jews who had come to accept Christianity turned to Hellenistic thought for categories which would enable them to articulate their personal and communal experience of God. Thus, the expression and amplification of their beliefs were influenced by Greek thinking. In reformulating their scriptural view of God philosophically they hoped to make it fully intelligible to themselves. At the same time they wanted to communicate with the Greek gentiles and to show them that their faith was fully compatible with reason. Thus, they carried out their theologizing with a view to satisfying the demands of philosophical speculation.[6]

Hartshorne has embarked on a similar undertaking in that what he has worked out is a conceptuality that aims to make sense of the religious idea of God just as what the early Christian Jews wished to formulate when they resorted to Hellenistic philosophy was a concept that fulfilled their demand for logical sense. That the combination of Jewish religious insights with Greek categories was, however, not entirely successful has led many to agree with Pascal that there is a vast difference between the God of the philosophers and the God of faith. It has also prompted Hartshorne to construct a concept of God which in his opinion reflects religious insights more faithfully.

This book examines Hartshorne's concept of God. For practical reasons it has been necessary to exclude his work on the proofs for the existence of God in spite of the difficulty of disassociating the problem of whether there is a God from the problem of how to conceive him. Besides, Hartshorne's justification for the belief in God's existence presupposes his concept of God. Moreover, if what has been said at the beginning is correct, then there is need to concentrate on the meaningfulness, as distinct from the reference, of our concept of God.

The book is composed of two parts. Part I discusses the approach adopted by Hartshorne. Inasmuch as he maintains that what he has worked out is based on the religious view, an analysis of the religious conception of God as Hartshorne interprets it is given at the outset. This is followed by a presentation of Hartshorne's understanding of metaphysics since it has a bearing on his approach to the problem and on the resulting concept of God. Part II consists of a number of chapters which present Hartshorne's attempt to provide a philosophical framework for this religious idea. His interpretation of God's perfection as worshipfulness and his doctrine of God's dipolarity, the distinction between the abstract and the concrete, between existence and actuality, and the Law of Polarity are analyzed in detail. Subsequent chapters take up the doctrine of dipolarity and show how Hartshorne rethinks our understanding of God's knowledge, power and goodness in the light of this doctrine. Related topics, such as divine knowledge and time, panentheism, the problem of evil, and immortality are also dealt with.

Throughout the writing of this book, I have had the assistance and encouragement of several people. Space does not permit me to mention all of them. However, I should like to record here my sincere gratitude to some of them, particularly to Charles Hartshorne. Not only did he generously give his time to discuss various points with me, but he has also kindly consented to write the postscript where he discusses some of the controversial aspects of his concept of God.

This study originated as part of a doctoral dissertation submitted to Trinity College, University of Dublin. It has been revised for publication. Certain sections have already appeared as parts of articles in *The Clergy Review* and *Milltown Studies*, and I am grateful to the editors of these journals for giving permission to reprint them here. Milltown Institute of Theology and Philosophy, Dublin, awarded me with a much appreciated Fellowship, which enabled me to concentrate on my research. Prof. John Gaskin, my Ph.D. supervisor, was most helpful during the early stages of this book. Former colleagues, especially Paul Lennon and the late John Kelly, and students of Milltown Institute provided me with opportunities to develop my ideas. The stimulating and challenging discussions I had with them helped to shape this work. My thanks are due to them and to many others who attended the courses, talks and papers which were based on this book and which I gave in various venues in Ireland and Britain.

The library staffs of the different universities and colleges where I did the research impressed me with their efficiency. I would like to thank them for getting my sources, some of which were not easily obtainable.

The editors and staff of Martinus Nijhoff deserve my gratitude. Their encouragement, patience and professionalism saw this work through to its present form.

Distance has been no barrier to the continued interest my mother and family have in my work. I am very much indebted to them for the many things, big and small, which they have done for me over the years. Finally and most of all, my wife, Marian, deserves my heartfelt thanks for her unfailing support and ever-present help. In addition, she has made suggestions and comments. This book is lovingly dedicated to her.

NOTES

1. Alfred North Whitehead wrote in *Religion in the Making* (New American Library, 1926), p. 66: "Today there is but one religious dogma in debate: What do you mean by "God"? And in this respect, today is like all its yesterdays. This is the fundamental religious dogma, and all other dogmas are subsidiary to it." Norman Pittenger, who quotes Whitehead in *Picturing God* (SCM Press, 1982), p. 1, maintains that what Whitehead said decades ago is just as valid today.

2. Quoted in Desmond Forristal, *The Mystery of God* (Dublin: Veritas Publications, 1980), p. 69.

3. Cf. H.P. Owen, *Concepts of Deity* (Macmillan, 1971), p. vii.

4. Anthony Flew puts this point forcefully. He argues that it is up to the theist to first introduce and defend his proposed concept of God and secondly, to provide sufficient reason for believing that this concept of his does have an application. Flew insists that the first of these stages needs to be emphasized even more strongly than the second. See his *The Presumption of Atheism and Other Essays* (London: Elek/Pemberton, 1976), p. 15.

5. Charles Hartshorne is widely recognized as a leading figure in process thought. The author of more than a dozen books and many articles, he taught in the Universities of Chicago, Emory and Texas at Austin. He has also lectured in different Asian and European centres of learning. For his biography and intellectual development, see, among others, "The Development of My Philosophy", Eugene H. Peters, *Hartshorne and Neoclassical Metaphysics: an Interpretation* (Lincoln: University of Nebraska Press, 1970).

   Process thought attempts to interpret reality in terms of *becoming* and *relativity*. This interpretation is based on the experience of the world as constantly changing and socially structured. For Hartshorne's account of the development of this movement, cf. "The Development of Process Philosophy". John Cobb traces the growth of process theology in chapter 2 of his *Process Theology as Political Theology* (Manchester University Press/Westminster Press, 1982). See also George R. Lucas, Jr., *The Genesis of Modern Process Thought: A*

Historical Outline with Bibliography (Metuchen, N.J. and London: Scarecrow Press, 1983). The quarterly journal *Process Studies* published in association with the Center for Process Studies at the School of Theology at Claremont, is an excellent source of developments in process thought. In addition to the Center for Process Studies at Claremont, there are similar centers in Louvain, Belgium, in Japan, and in Tübingen, Germany.

6. Cf. H.P. Owen, *op. cit.*, p. 1.

PART I

HARTSHORNE'S APPROACH

CHAPTER 1

THE RELIGIOUS TERM "GOD"

I. Religion as Source

In this chapter we shall investigate Hartshorne's analysis of the religious term "God". This investigation is called for because any attempt to sketch out Hartshorne's concept of God should first give an account of his interpretation of the religious idea of God since what he has tried to do is to provide us with a more satisfactory framework for articulating what religion means by God. Hartshorne himself regards religion as the starting point and the frame of reference of the philosophical stand which he has taken and developed[1] while persistently claiming that classical theism has misrepresented religious insights. One must, therefore, start with the source, i.e. religion, rather than with its philosophical development.

Hartshorne's interpretation of the religious idea of God is found scattered throughout his writings and is particularly noticeable when he is arguing his case for what he calls "dipolar theism", a phrase which will be explained later. However, in this chapter, what will be of primary concern to us is his presentation of the "God" of religion rather than his dipolar theism. Hartshorne is not a comparative religionist. So this exposition of the religious idea of God as Hartshorne apprehends it will follow the way he states it in various writings.

Religion, he declares, is intuitive in origin and the philosophical task is to find logical patterns appropriate to express this intuition.[2] For Hartshorne then the religious idea of God is an intuitive or pre-philosophical grasp of who God is. But one is immediately aware of difficulties attending such a claim. Religion is very much associated with philosophy and its development is, to some extent, due to that discipline. Hartshorne himself points out that high religions came into maturity only after the rise of philosophy.[3] There has always been a close link between the two. Clearly, it is not a simple proposition to disentangle religion from its philosophical attachments and to come up with a pre-philosophical idea of God. Nonetheless, Hartshorne believes that one can arrive at the kernel of religion, and at the religious idea of God, regardless of any philosophy. It is possible, so to speak, to push aside as far as we can philosophical trappings so as to examine the claims of religion in their non-philosophical or pre-philosophical state.[4]

Hartshorne insists that we must "allow religion to speak for itself" before we concern ourselves with its philosophical expression because religion has played a large, if not decisive, part in the shaping of our concept of God. So despite the fact that philosophy does not argue from revealed premises, it does turn at times to religion to furnish the material. Philosophy tries to develop further issues raised by religion "If," Hartshorne writes, "the task is to form a rational theory about the central religious idea, the idea of God, it seems proper to begin by asking religion, including revealed religion, what it means by "God".[5] Unfortunately, in Hartshorne's view, this has been overlooked in many cases, not least in discussions centered on the idea of God. While it has been recognized that religion and philosophy have influenced each other, it has not always been admitted that religion itself is truly a source of religious philosophizing. For this reason Hartshorne distinguishes what he calls "the religious strand" from "the theological (or philosophical strand)".[6] It is the religious strand that ought to be the source for our understanding of the "God" of religion.

Hartshorne's suggestion for greater fidelity to religion and its claims is also reflected in his statement — which appears to be a main tenet of his — that basic ideas derive somehow from direct experience or intuition, life as concretely lived.[7] Thus, if one wished to trace the roots of abstract ideas, one will find them in concrete experiencing of various kinds.[8] An analysis of the religious idea of God ought therefore to concentrate on these aspects of experience generally known as religious. No doubt, there are widely different religious experiences as borne out by the conflicting claims of the different religions. Still, in so far as the idea of God is distinguishable from others, Hartshorne is convinced that there must be privileged experiences which particularly serve to give it meaning — irrespective of whether or not they suffice to prove its truth.[9] He argues that one could reasonably assume that an intuitive or experiential basis for a religious idea would be in some actual religion or religions and that it is there that this intuition comes most forcibly into consciousness. Any philosophical formulation of a religious insight has thus to be tested as to whether it in fact expresses the content of religion in its higher manifestation.[10]

But before we look at the "God" of religion let us find out first what constitutes religion. The content or essence of religion, as far as Hartshorne is concerned, is worship. Accordingly, he defines religion as "devoted love for a being regarded as superlatively worthy of love". He agrees with Tillich that the great commandment to love God with all one's being amounts to a definition of worship. Although this formulation sounds Christian, Hartshorne claims that it also sums up the beliefs of the other higher religions since they too are concerned with loving God totally.

As we shall see later, this definition of religion as worship serves as the basis for Hartshorne's analysis of the religious idea of God. But it is worth noting now that it also draws attention to a certain understanding of man's nature. Man, as Hartshorne sees him, is but a fragment of reality.[12] His existence is regarded as only one among many, hence, he is to some degree comparable to a mere grain of sand or a passing speck of dust. Like them, he is limited in space and time and in every other way. ("Fragmentary" is the term preferred by Hartshorne to "finite" to describe man's nature since for Hartshorne God too has a finite aspect but is not fragmentary.) We are merely fragments of finite reality, not the whole of it, since each of us is but one localized being among others whereas God in his finitude is the whole of finite reality. God, and only God, cannot be a fragment of anything else. Thus, to say that all creatures including man, are finite is to say too little. One should describe them as not merely finite but fragmentary, mere parts of the whole of reality. In short, not finitude but fragmentariness is the mark of the non-divine.[13]

It is man's reaction to this fragmentariness which characterizes his religion. A man's religion is good if he accepts his relative insignificance in the best possible way. It is poor or non-existent if he closes his eyes to his situation, persuading himself that his limitation in space and time is only of slight importance or if he considers himself the center of the universe, with everything else revolving around him, or if he regards a particular group – family, class, race – as that universe to which he should devote his entire attention. All of these reactions are, in one way or another, a non-acceptance of man's fragmentary nature. Hartshorne considers this self-deification by man a chief rival in our time of what he considers to be true religion.[14]

The two parts of the definition of religion as worship, i.e. total love for God and man's acceptance of his fragmentariness, are thus related to each other. True worship is achieved only when man humbly accepts his fragmentary status. Non-worship is either a forgetfulness or a denial of man's real situation. Yet man is not debased even if the emphasis on man's fragmentariness apparently points towards something outside man giving him significance and may convey the impression that man in himself has very little importance, if any at all. Worship is *loving* God with all one's being. It is in the context of love that Hartshorne talks of worship and therefore, far from degrading man, it enables him to become aware of some significance in his fragmentariness. We are or can be loving "fragments". We are also loved, called upon to enter a particular relationship with God. Thus, worship is actually an enhancement of ourselves and of the universe.[15]

Having explained what constitutes true religion, Hartshorne then suggests that we consult two sources which he considers as embodying what is essential in the religious understanding of God.[16] The first source is what is technically classified as revelation, for instance, the Scriptures – Hindu, Chinese, Mohammedan, Christian, etc. – and the official creeds of the various churches. In citing these as a source, Hartshorne is aware that they may still show philosophical influences, seeing that even the notion of revelation has philosophical overtones. Moreover, some of those who were responsible for committing the revealed word to writing were philosophically inclined. As well as that, a number of creeds of the different religions are expressed philosophically. In this context, one thinks readily of the idea of "substance" in the longer christian creed. But Hartshorne argues that in the biblical writings, at least, there is little philosophy of the technical sort and not much in the more popular creeds, such as the Apostles' creed.

The second source of the religious idea of God are recognized functions and attitudes, such as prayer, sense of sin, salvation and so on. Hartshorne explains that the idea of God first reaches vivid consciousness in an emotional and practical rather than in an explicitly logical or analytic form. This initial awareness of God is not particularly simple since it is found amidst a wealth of expression (which is often highly poetic, and not wholly consistent) of feelings and imperatives of behaviour. Simultaneously, there is a relative absence of definition, analysis or demonstration. But where there is a dearth of definiteness, there is by way of compensation a richness of insight into the fundamental experiences from which a meaningful idea of God can be derived.[17] Together with the first source, these experiences should give us a glimpse into how religion conceives God.

II. "God" in Religion

What emerges from an examination of these sources is the recognition of God as the worshipful one. In theistic religions God is the one who is worshipped, the adequate object of unstinted or wholehearted devotion, of unlimited love.[18] Yet Hartshorne insists that, in spite of the fact that he consults religious sources, he is not working his way from an empirical fact, i.e. the fact *that* some people worship or have "religious experience". It is not the *fact* but the *idea* of worship from which he derives the definition of "God" as the worshipful one. This is because no one can ascertain whether there really is someone who loves God or anything else in a manner which would fit the description "with all one's being". However, we can understand the *idea* of such a complete devotion and God as the appropriate recipient of such an ideal devotion.[19]

To regard God as the worshipful one is to imply his all-inclusiveness. This follows from the meaning of worship as total love. If God is loved or can be loved with all one's capacities, then he must in some sense coincide with being or reality itself. He must, furthermore, be the universal object of every interest or every attachment. That is to say, our love for anything or anyone includes God. Only if God is all-inclusive can devotion to him be total. We can love God with *all* our being only if God is said to be in everything and everything to be in God. Since worship entails finding the entire meaning of life, all its values, in relation to the one worshipped, it has significance only if any love, interest or devotion which one may have is part of one's love for God. Thus, the second part of the great commandment, that we are to love our neighbors as ourselves, is actually an explication of the same commandment. It is not an additional command. Loving our neighbor *is* loving God as any love of neighbor or of ourselves must already be embraced in our relationship with God. The very love which we bear for another being is in reality love of God.[20]

Hartshorne defends his position that "all-inclusiveness" is a religious concept by showing that it is a fairly clear and direct implication in the teachings of at least three religions. Judaism, Christianity and Islam, he believes, would agree with the conception of worship embodied in the commandment, "thou shalt love the Lord thy God with all thy heart and with all thy mind and with all thy soul and with all thy strength". The idea of wholeness in our response is plainly stated here in that the word "all" reiterated four times indicates that every response, every aspect of it, must be a way of loving God.[21]

It should be noted in passing that for Hartshorne the religious belief in an all-inclusive reality does not necessarily border on pantheism, unless all that is meant by this term is a doctrine that teaches that the divine includes all things. Pantheism in its historical setting is generally construed in such a way that human freedom is thought of as merely illusory. Religion, on the other hand, regards human freedom as genuine yet being free does not stop creatures from being integrated in God.[22] Pantheism, historically considered, also equates God with the world; God and the world are one. Religion dissociates itself from such a view. What it holds is that God contains the world but is not the world. The world is somehow in God, but in some way he is also distinct from it.[23]

Such an all-inclusive reality must somehow be one; he cannot simply be another, even a supreme, reality in addition to other realities. There can be no gods besides God. There can be nothing beside, outside, or merely additional to him. For if there were, there would have to be an additional interest, love or devotion. This would prevent anyone from loving God with *all one's being*. Hence, Hartshorne is not surprised that religion believes in one God: God's oneness correlative to the integrity of response is a Jewish-Christian-Islamic tenet.[24]

Religion also describes God as unsurpassable or superior to everything else.[25] It tends to maximize whatever we affirm of God; hence, God is known as "the supreme reality", exalted beyond all that we can conceive, unsurpassable by anyone or anything. Again this is entailed by God's worshipfulness; if he is worshipful, he must not be conceivably surpassed by another. It would be inconsistent to worship someone who is not above everyone or everything else. In addition, worship points to a radical asymmetry in the relations between God and his worshippers. They worship him, he does not worship them; they do not judge him whereas he does judge them. They presuppose him as the cause of their existence while the reverse does not apply. As Hartshorne himself puts it, "only radical inequality can justify worship, and relations of inequality are non-symmetrical; if X is superior to Y, Y is not superior but inferior to X".[26] Strictly speaking then, we cannot worship a fellow creature although towards him, her or it we may have feelings of wonder, awe and gratitude, feelings which are normally associated with worship. Only an all-inclusive reality could be the proper object of worship for only he could be "loved with all one's being".

God's unsurpassability is exemplified in his goodness. Not only is God supremely lovable, he is considered love itself. The idea of worship as loving God with all one's being is linked in religion with the idea that he whom we are thus asked to love wholly is himself also love, the divine love for all creatures and for himself as including all. *Deus est caritas* is a common religious teaching.[27] Certainty of the world-embracing love of God is in fact considered to be the most religious attitude, coupled with a life lived accordingly and is the reason why God is to be loved in a personal way, as one, for example, loves a parent or a friend. He is not to be loved merely as a mathematician loves a beautiful piece of reasoning, or as a philosopher may love his ideas. God is said to be the supremely loving individual, who loves us not just by unintentionally causing benefits to the creatures, as the rain or sun does, but with conscious appreciation of or concern for their happiness.[28] The God of religion is one of understanding and sympathy, and one to whom creatures could appeal, the all-loving and supremely efficacious friend of man and all other creatures. Furthermore, God's goodness is never changing; his love for us remains steadfast (we shall see later on that this is, in Hartshorne's view, what is meant by God's absoluteness). We can always rely on him no matter in what state we find ourselves. He is a friend to friend and foe alike. This is not to say, however, that to worship the all-good God means that no harm will befall the worshipper. There is no absolute security against suffering; but God's goodness is such that in the face of suffering, we can still count on him. The security or confidence that worshippers have is directed towards this unchanging and unrivaled goodness of God.

God's unsurpassability can also be seen in the way religion understands God's power. He is considered to be supremely powerful, thereby rendering him superior to everyone else. In several great religions, God is thought of as an agent or active individual definitely exalted above every other agent. He is supreme, and he exercises a controlling power.[29] But while this belief is clearly upheld by high religions, there is, as Hartshorne sees it, vagueness in their description of God as a "creator" other than that he contributes maximally and productively to every stage of reality. The Hindus, for instance, seem to have been little concerned with the idea of a beginning of reality in time; the book of Genesis, according to some scholars at least, is not clear on this point while the New Testament has little to say about it.[30]

When religion refers to God's knowledge, it assumes that God knows the truth in the sense in which we do not. We know something like the truth whereas God *knows* the truth. Religion equates God's knowledge with the truth so much so that one could literally say that the truth is what God knows, and what God knows is the truth. It is the one knowledge which coincides with the truth. Thus, to say that God knows that I am innocent is another way of saying that I am innocent.[31]

Religion, however, is not so emphatic about the absoluteness of God's happiness.[32] In fact, we are told that God is displeased by sin. Consequently, he cannot be described as being absolutely happy when someone has sinned. We also hear that God sympathizes with us. He loves us even to the point of suffering with us. He wishes to alleviate our suffering. Moreover, there is much talk in religious circles about serving God and carrying out his plans, all to his greater honour and glory. From all this, we can conclude that we do contribute to God's state of happiness. This is exactly what religion believes in, insists Hartshorne. It is a belief which though expressed in an anthropomorphic way clearly shows that religion is concerned with God's relationship with man as well as man's relationship with him. Religion makes it its business to enhance the interaction between God and man. Any basic aspect of religious practice exhibits this divine-human reciprocity as essential. There is talk of sacrifice and serving God precisely because the basic religious view is that man's good acts and happiness have a value to God, which his bad acts and misery do not have. Love, in this particular context, means

16

happiness that varies somehow with the changes in the beloved. Since God is love, he cannot remain unmoved by the attempts of his worshippers to please him. Likewise, he cannot but be saddened by their misery and sin.

This presentation of Hartshorne's understanding of the religious idea of God has been carried out here as if there were only one such idea. With some qualification, Hartshorne believes this to be the case with higher religions (excluded from his consideration are primitive religions). In them we shall find a somewhat definite, coherent, and universal idea: the religious meaning of "God", or Ishvara in Sanskrit, Allah in Arabic, or the Holy One of Israel. This analysis of the religious understanding of God concentrated on what was common to the higher religions, hence, it was by necessity rather general. Hartshorne draws upon the higher religions for that idea which in his estimation is most susceptible to logical handling, i.e. the most sharply and consistently definable. The fundamental idea which he finds common at least to Judaism, Christianity and Islam, at their best, and with more or less close analogues in some forms of Hinduism and Buddhism (in spite of what is often said of the latter) is the idea of God as the worshipful one, who is all-inclusive, one and unsurpassable in his goodness, power and knowledge but whose happiness is affected by others.[33] It is this understanding of 'God' which Hartshorne proposes to develop in his philosophy.

NOTES

1. For instance, in the Preface to his book, CSPM, p. xviii, he writes: "From an early pious — yet rather liberal — Christian training, my dogmatic slumber which was rudely and once for all interrupted by Matthew Arnold's *Literature and Dogma*, the firmest residuum is summed up in the phrase *Deus est caritas*, together with the two "Great Commandments": total love for God, and love for neighbors comparable to love for self. But at least something like these principles is in certain forms of Hinduism, Buddhism, Judaism, Islam, Zoroastrianism, and even in the two-thousand-year-old hymns of Ikhnaton. If there are central intuitive convictions back of my acceptance or rejection of philosophical doctrines, these may be the ones." As discussed in the text of this chapter these are the principles which constitute religion for Hartshorne.
2. Cf. "The God of Religion and the God of Philosophy", p. 161. In this article, Hartshorne expresses this point as a hypothesis. That this is, however, his own approach is clear from his other writings. See, for example, his MV, p. x and pp. 85 – 141; "Twelve Elements of my Philosophy", pp. 7 – 15.
3. MV, p. 91.
4. It should be noted here that the analysis is not intended to be an assumptionless one. Hartshorne believes that because of the social character of experience, "there can be no wholly non-speculative descriptions of the given, somewhat as there is no such thing as mere assembling of facts prior to the formation of hypothesis in natural science". "The Develop-

ment of my Philosophy'', p. 215. One starts with beliefs, but beliefs which are pre-philosophical. As has been pointed out, it is Hartshorne's thesis that the philosophical tenets on religion as heretofore understood do not give due consideration to the claims of religion.

5. "Can There be Proofs for the Existence of God?", p. 62.
6. MV, pp. x, 134 – 137.
7. NTOT, p. 2.
8. Cf. CSPM, p. 75.
9. MV, p. 86.
10. "Criteria for Ideas of God", p. 90. Religious experiences, however, should not form the main reason for concluding that God exists since the mere *claim* to perceive or experience God is hardly a rational justification, in the normal sense. "A Philosopher's Assessment of Christianity", p. 173.
11. MV, p. 3.
12. "Man's Fragmentariness", p. 17; "Significance of Man in the Life of God", p. 40.
13. "The Idea of a Worshipful Being", p. 165.
14. "The Modern World and the Modern View of God", p. 73.
15. This point is well discussed by David R. Mason in his "An Examination of "Worship" as a Key for Re-examining the God-Problem", *Journal of Religion*, LV, 1955, pp. 76 – 94. Mason elaborates on Hartshorne's use of worship in the context of love and argues that such a conception is far from abasing man. Rather, worship as love enhances self, fellow-creatures and God.

Of course, not every kind of worship falls within the scope of Hartshorne's definition. There are many forms of worship: noble, ignoble, primitive, sophisticated, superstitious, idolatrous, relatively enlightened and so forth, which Hartshorne lists. With each form of worship a different conception of God comes to the fore. The object of primitive worship, for instance, is a mere superhuman while that of superstitious worship is a magical God. Consequently, Hartshorne's definition of worship is intended to exclude these. Hartshorne therefore offers this extended definition: "worship is the *integrating* of all one's thoughts and purposes, all valuations and meanings, all perceptions and conceptions". NTOT, pp. 4 – 5. Consciousness is the added element here. To worship is to do something consciously. It is to respond with awareness to the situations described above. With this definition, man's response to his fragmentary nature is seen as being lifted to the level of explicit awareness. The more consciousness there is, the more completely the ideal of worship is realized. Such an account of worship would distinguish it from other forms just mentioned since these lack the element of consciousness.

16. MV, pp. 91 – 92.
17. PSG, p. 1.
18. NTOT, p. 3; "The Two Possible Philosophical Definitions of God", p. 121; "Can There be Proofs for the Existence of God?", p. 62. Hartshorne's claim that higher religions regard God as the Worshipful One can be found in many of his writings. See, for example, "The Idea of God – Literal or Analogical", p. 131; "Two Strata of Meaning in Religious Discourse", p. 5. He excludes primitive religions and polytheistic religions due to their very crudely anthropomorphic approach. Religion refers to the higher religions, i.e. Judaism, Christianity, Islam, some forms of Hinduism, and of Buddhism, in their common element.

The Worshipful One should not, however, be identified unquestioningly with "God" as traditionally conceived to be. In Hartshorne's mind, the idea of God which has been the center of much talk was often the imputed object of some deceptive substitute of worship. This is why he says that not only is the "God of religion" different from the "God of philosophy", but it is not the "God of theology", either (at least in the traditional sense since traditional theology has equated God with the Absolute). Hartshorne adds that what Pascal called the "God of the Philosophers" is, strictly speaking, the God of one stage in the development of the philosophical (which Hartshorne calls the "classical") idea of God. His contention is that the "God of neo-classical philosophy" comes closer to what religion means by "God". Cf. "Two Forms of Idolatry", pp. 5 – 7; also "Interview", pp. 1 – 2.

19. "Can There be Proofs…", p. 62. In reply to Bultman's query as to how we derive the idea of God, Hartshorne writes that this is done in several ways. "The recognition of ourselves as beings surpassable by others in power, wisdom, duration and other positive traits yields, by simple contrast, that of the being *un*surpassable by others. "God" is the name for the one who is unsurpassable by any conceivable being other than himself." He continues, "From the understanding of "surpassable by others" one derives, by mere negation, the idea of "unsurpassable by others"". Then he goes on to say that one can also derive the idea of God "from the idea of worship as such". What he means is that "if we could conceive a superior to God we should either have to worship that superior, were it only a mere possibility, or else find ourselves unable to worship at all". NTOT, pp. 128 – 130.

20. LP, pp. 40 – 41.

21. NTOT, pp. 7 – 8.

22. At this stage what is of interest is not *how* religion explains this paradoxical doctrine but merely *that* it holds both tenets. Later on it will be shown how Hartshorne tries in his philosophy to make sense of God's all-inclusiveness *and* man's freedom.

23. Accordingly, Hartshorne develops a "panentheistic" conception of God.

24. "Idea of God – Literal or Analogical?", p. 131. Even the doctrine of the Trinity, Hartshorne says, is not intended to contradict the belief in God's oneness. Cf. NTOT, p. 8.

25. NTOT, p. 14f.; also MV, p. 92f. The term itself (unsurpassability) is, I think, Hartshornian rather than religious. The idea is, however, part of religious belief in that the different religions definitely regard God to be unrivaled. Hartshorne hesitates to use the word "perfect" even if religion does because he believes that the connotation of that term does not match the religious understanding of God's superiority. This point will be discussed further in chapter 3.

26. "The Two Possible Definitions of God", p. 121.

27. MV, pp. xiv, 89.

28. "The God of Religion and the God of Philosophy", p. 134.

29. *Ibid.*, p. 152.

30. MV, pp. 93 – 94.

31. "Interview", p. 4.

32. MV, p. 94; also "Process Philosophy as a Resource for Christian Thought", pp. 44f.

33. "Two Forms of Idolatry", p. 4; "The God of Religion and the God of Philosophy", p. 161.

CHAPTER 2

HARTSHORNE'S METHOD

I. Metaphysics

In his attempt to supply us with a philosophical framework for understanding more faithfully what religion means by God, Hartshorne adopts a meta-physical approach. To come to grips then with what he has in mind, it is essential to probe into Hartshorne's interpretation of metaphysics. In CSPM[1] he offers several definitions; but for our present purposes, it will be sufficient to cite and discuss only a few of these, especially since Hartshorne himself maintains that his definitions overlap and that they differ among themselves only in emphasis. Another reason for examining what metaphysics means for Hartshorne is his insistence that it is metaphysical knowledge which enables us to know God literally and positively. Later in this chapter, we shall see why Hartshorne makes this claim and how he justifies it.

Metaphysics, according to Hartshorne, is the study of the general features of experience.[2] This definition in some ways resembles that given by White-head: metaphysics is "the endeavour to frame a coherent, logical, necessary system of *general ideas in terms of which every element of our experience can be interpreted*".[3] One of the first points which will be noticed in Hartshorne's definition is that metaphysics is not, as is sometimes mistakenly conceived to be, the study of what is wholly transcendent or supersensible. It implies that what is metaphysical is not behind or above the physical or the observable but applies to the physical and the observable as well as everything else. He has affirmed in many of his writings that the pursuit of metaphysical ideas is rooted in experience and the analysis that metaphysicians conduct is related to experience. Hence, it is misleading to think of metaphysicians as seeking the object of their study "behind" the objects of empirical science, if by this is meant that in their search for the ultimate causes of things or for essences, metaphysicians are looking for something over and above experience.

But what distinguishes metaphysics from other disciplines which likewise take experience as their starting point is its search for *strict generality or universality*. Unlike other disciplines, metaphysics examines the extremely general features of experience or its universal traits. It is the attempt to clarify those ideas or truths which are so general that no conceivable facts and no conceivable observations could fail to illustrate them.[4] By virtue of this generality, metaphysical ideas or truths are said always to be embodied in experience; that is, they are exemplified in every experience. It is claimed, therefore, that any experience must not only be compatible with these metaphysical ideas or truths, but it must also corroborate them. As Hartshorne puts it, "Metaphysical truths may be described as such that no experience can contradict them, but also such that any experience must illustrate them".[5] Hartshorne cites as an example the truth, which he maintains is metaphysical, that "the present is always influenced by the past". No possible experience could come into conflict with it since we cannot know that we are uninfluenced by the past. To know the past is already to be influenced in one's state of knowledge by it.[6] When Hartshorne therefore states that metaphysics is the study of the general features of experience, he means not only that metaphysical ideas are derived from experience but also that they are so general that they are said to be applicable to every experience, actual or possible.

This extension of the study of truly general features to include possible experience leads Hartshorne to underscore another characteristic of metaphysics: the search for *necessary* truths. These truths are necessary in that, unlike empirical truths or facts, they cannot be otherwise since they are about what is common to all possible facts. They are not just about this world but about reality in general, about any and all possibilities for a world. Hartshorne maintains that the validity of metaphysical ideas is, in principle, for all cosmic epochs.[7]

Consequently, the metaphysical search is more than the mere observation of reality (the method used by empirical sciences) since observation only shows what goes on in the actual world with its particular regularities or natural laws. Observation does not and cannot show what must go on or what principles would be valid in any viable, truly possible world. Metaphysics, on the other hand, tries to study what cuts across such differentiation and hence is necessarily true. To accomplish this one must go beyond mere observation. Another method is called for.

So far, Hartshorne's definition of metaphysics as the study of the general features of experience shows us that metaphysical ideas or truths are extremely generalized and therefore are necessary truths about actual *and* conceivable reality. These truths originate from and are based on our experience of what is.

Hartshorne gives us another indication of what he means by metaphysics in his examination of the nature of metaphysical judgments.[8] He stresses that metaphysical judgments are *existential*, i.e. they are about our experience of what exists. But they are *necessary* existential judgments in that they cannot be otherwise. Insofar as they are necessary, they cannot be opposed by facts. Instead, facts illustrate and confirm metaphysical judgments. Furthermore, such judgments apply to all actual as well as possible states of affairs. In other words, they are universal. It is this universality which makes them necessary since what is true of *all* reality *must* be true. For this reason Hartshorne sees a very close link between universality and necessity. In claiming that metaphysical truths are non-particularized or universal, he is at the same time characterizing them as necessary. Although a statement such as "something exists" may assert the existence of something particular (e.g. "something" could refer to the table beside me) as a strictly generalized statement it is not restricted to any one particular object. And because it applies to everything and anything, it cannot but be true. It is, therefore, necessary.

However, it is in all cases only probable that we have approximated to a correct understanding of necessary truth.[9] This is why in another sense, metaphysical judgments are understood to be *synthetic*. Granted that the most general ideas cannot possibly be untrue, it is nevertheless possible that we have confusedly grasped their meaning. Mistakes can occur. Thus, unlike mathematics, metaphysics does not claim absolute certainty. The results arrived at in a metaphysical inquiry lack the definiteness of purely mathematical ideas. This is not to say, however, that they lack definiteness altogether. To put it in another way, while a metaphysical judgment seeks to express something which is universally and necessarily true, our grasp of that truth may not always be correct. But this merely means that what we took to be a metaphysical truth turns out not to be so. For this reason the metaphysical inquiry is an on-going process, a search, to discover what is universally and necessarily true.

The universality and necessity of metaphysical statements are further highlighted by Hartshorne when he characterizes them as *completely non-restrictive* in opposition to *partially restrictive* and to *completely restrictive statements*. A metaphysical statement like "something exists" excludes nothing and is verified every moment. That is to say, in no conceivable circumstance is the statement "something exists" falsifiable. Its necessity lies in that it is implied by any and every proposition. *Partially restrictive* statements, on the other hand, are contingent. If they are affirmative, they also implicitly deny something. If they are negative, they also implicitly affirm something. Hartshorne offers as example the statement "There are men in the room". According to him, this factual statement affirms the presence of men in the room while implicitly denying that the room is filled solid from floor to ceiling with non-human bodies. Its negation "There are no men in the room" denies the presence of men but at the same time it affirms by implication that every substantial part of the room contains something, if only air or a "vacuum" furnishing free passage to radiant energy, other than men.

The third class of statements, which Hartshorne calls *completely restrictive*, deny that any existential possibility is realized. If, for instance, one asserted that "nothing exists", one would be excluding anything and everything. Hartshorne argues that such a statement could not conceivable be verified since the verifying experience itself must exist. Nor can anyone experience bare nothing. But such a statement can be falsified. In fact, we falsify it every moment and thus show that it is untrue that "nothing exists". A completely restrictive statement, therefore, is not verifiable, but it is falsifiable. As a wholly negative statement, it expresses an impossibility and not just a conceivable but unrealized fact.

While completely restrictive statements like "nothing exists" are not verifiable but falsifiable, completely non-restrictive, i.e. metaphysical, statements are unfalsifiable. A statement is truly metaphysical if it cannot be falsified by experience. Hartshorne adopts and adapts Karl Popper's argument that a hypothesis is scientific if it can be observationally falsified, not if it can be verified. It is doubtful, Hartshorne explains, if strictly speaking any scientific generalization has been verified in the sense that it has been shown to be true exactly as it stands. The really crucial experiments are not those which stand a chance of proving some theory but those which can disprove it. As Hartshorne puts it, "one instance clearly not in accordance with a supposed law refutes the law, but many instances in conformity with the law still do not prove it".[10] He supports Popper's view that falsification rather than direct verification is the more viable criterion. He adds that this is true even in metaphysics although here falsification must be *a priori*, that is, by discovering absurdity and not merely by showing a conflict with fact.[11]

What has been said up to this point reveals that Hartshorne does not agree that all existential statements (or all positive generalizations) are contingent or factual. For, as we have seen, metaphysical statements are existential but not factual; they are necessary and not contingent. In spite of the fact that they state nothing factual or contingent, they do say something true about actual and possible reality. Metaphysical statements do not describe particular things. What they do is express what is common to, or true of, every reality. This is why they are implicit in any description of anything. They convey nothing new (except perhaps to make us more conscious of what is merely implicit). We become more aware of what never fails to be present in experience, even though not distinctly attended to.

Hartshorne then understands metaphysical knowledge to be based on and to be derived from experience. But how does one arrive at such a generalized knowledge? In Hartshorne's view, it is not necessary to have all possible experiences but only some experiences coupled with the capacity to abstract or explicitly universalize. What creates problems for the would-be metaphysician is not the process of generalization since even outside of metaphysics we are prone to engage in it. The real difficulty in the kind of generalization demanded in metaphysics is in distinguishing metaphysical concepts from non-metaphysical ones. Hartshorne explains this point by contrasting metaphysics with natural science both of which make generalizations. In natural science one pays attention to the details of experience and then generalizes these details so as to arrive at the total system of details which distinguish the actual world from conceivable ones. In metaphysics, on the other hand, one turns to the generic traits of human experience which one then generalizes in order to arrive at the generic traits of all experience, actual and possible, and from here to discover the abiding features of the entire cosmos.[12]

As has been mentioned earlier, errors can and do occur in metaphysics.[13] This is because what metaphysics aims to achieve is much more extensive. Sometimes an allegedly metaphysical statement may really be empirical in which case it is conceivable that some experiences would be incompatible with that statement. In Hartshorne's view, the failure to grasp metaphysical meaning or truth involves either the defect of vagueness or the defect of inconsistency. Thus, it is helpful, even if not always efficacious, to relate metaphysical ideas into a system in which each concept helps to define and is partly defined by all others.[14] However, the metaphysician ought not only to strive after systematic coherence but he must also refer his metaphysical claims back to experience to test their generality. In this task, one can seek the aid of natural science in that it can discredit generalizations which one is claiming to be applicable to all time and all existence. Natural science can bring up instances which would falsify such rather hasty conclusions.[15] Therefore, it is important for these ideas not just to be coherently linked up but also to be adequate to other experiences, i.e. not to be falsified by them. If they are falsified, then these ideas are not really metaphysical.

The challenge of fulfilling the criteria of *coherence* and *adequacy* makes metaphysical inquiry difficult indeed. Hartshorne notes that even if we can suppose the existence of metaphysical truths, it does not follow that man's knowledge and expression of these truths can ever possess such adequacy as to rule out further progress in our metaphysical pursuit. He observes that, "man's grasp of the absolute is not absolute; it is not an affair of all or nothing but of degree".[16] Hence, he holds on to a distinction between our

metaphysical pursuit or analysis and the metaphysical truths or ideas themselves. For him there can be no absolutely satisfactory and final metaphysical
analysis.

The contribution that can be made by natural science to the discovery of
metaphysical ideas has already been pointed out: natural science helps to
ensure the adequacy of metaphysical truths. According to Hartshorne, logic
is also an ally. He regards logic as the search for alternatives, the exploration
of the possibility of formulating an alternative to one's initial ideas or statement. In a way the initial idea or statement is a hypothesis which has to be
tested. By discovering a logically complete classification of possible ideas,
one can avoid a question – begging procedure. In this respect mathematics
too is useful because through mathematically possible combinations the
definiteness and completeness of the possibilities can be certified even though
these mathematically possible combinations cannot establish the truth of that
statement. Hartshorne brings out the importance of conducting a mathematical survey of possibilities by making the observation that men do not
adopt philosophical positions because they are beyond question nor because
conclusions are deemed to be completely satisfactory but because they seem
to be stronger or more satisfactory than alternative positions. It is, he thinks,
a matter of preference and not of absolute sun-clear evidence and perfect
understanding.[17]

So while Hartshorne takes the data from experience (practical, ethical,
aesthetic and religious) as the basis of his metaphysics, he turns to formal
logic and mathematics to achieve coherence and clarity in his metaphysical
analysis. In his opinion, in spite of the obscurity of metaphysical ideas, they
can be given a certain definiteness by means of an analysis such as one will
find in formal logic and mathematics. An important step in the reasoning
process that will lead to metaphysical ideas is therefore making an exhaustive
survey of possible standpoints and then eliminating those which are seen to be
false. The success of this process depends finally on how exhaustive one's survey is.[18] Hartshorne draws our attention to what he calls three-cornered
thinking, according to which one asks whether something is true in *all*
respects, in *some* respects or in *none*. A good example of this three-cornered
thinking is the way Hartshorne handles the problem concerning our concepts
of God (which we shall have occasion to take up in more detail in chapter
three). For instance, he asks whether one should regard God as perfect *in all
ways*, in *some ways*, or in *no* way. He then discusses each of these possibilities, ruling out those which are untenable.

The importance laid by Hartshorne on the search for alternatives through
logic and mathematics in arriving at metaphysical concepts is in contrast with

his caution in taking axioms to be metaphysical truths without subjecting them to close scrutiny. As far as he is concerned, axioms serve a certain function, but they too have to be tested. In philosophy axioms should have no standing unless and until the possibility has been seriously considered that they are at best merely plausible rather than genuinely self-evident and certain. The significance of axioms can be exaggerated, especially when it is held that we learn the truth of propositions by deducing them from initial propositions called axioms which are themselves known to be true by intuitive self-evidence or by induction. It is fallacious to regard deduction as merely exploiting truth already discovered but not helping in its discovery. For Hartshorne, deduction is "a way of magnifying the testability of assumptions, rather than simply a way of magnifying their importance and meaning once tested".[19] Deduction then is not just a method of deriving truths from already established propositions but should also be regarded as a way of testing those same propositions or axioms. This is not to say that Hartshorne is advocating a presuppositionless approach to metaphysics. In fact, he criticizes Husserl for having a naïve Cartesian confidence concerning the possibility of being absolutely clear about phenomenological reports. To Hartshorne obstacles to such clarity and certainty are to some extent insuperable. But in so far as it is possible to overcome them the way to do it is not through "bracketing the world" but through other ways, notably by trying out various logically possible formulations of what experience may be thought to be, looking to direct experience for illustrations.[20]

Aside from logical analysis and his own experience (both of which have already been discussed), the metaphysician has in intellectual history an additional resource in his search for authentically metaphysical concepts. History itself shows that analytic capacity is seldom so adequate than one can afford to neglect what others have already done in the past. One seldom has the wit and patience to master the conceptual possibilities without having to take the trouble of finding out what others who have already taken seriously some of the possible ways of thinking about basic problems have said or written on the subject.[21] For this reason open-mindedness to the views of others should characterize the metaphysical search. There ought to be free, fair and honest dialogue with them since we cannot really be completely free of bias, either.[22]

By way of summing up this discussion of Hartshorne's understanding of metaphysics, we can say that for Hartshorne metaphysics starts from and is rooted in experience. It differs from other experiential disciplines, however, because it is a search through a process of abstraction and logical analysis for what is extremely general about experience. If we are successful, then the kind of truths we obtain will be universal and necessary.

II. Our Knowledge of God

According to Hartshorne, metaphysics enables us to make certain claims about God. This is because God in Hartshorne's metaphysical scheme is not considered an exception to metaphysical principles or truths but an exemplification. In this section we shall see why and to what extent Hartshorne includes God within his metaphysical system. We shall do this by investigating how his conception of metaphysics has a bearing on the way he describes God.

In his God-talk Hartshorne acknowledges different ways of speaking of God: *symbolic, literal (or formal)* and *analogical.* One is talking of God in a symbolic way when one calls God a rock, a king, a ruler, a shepherd or a parent. Hartshorne also calls this kind of predication "material" because the implied comparison is in terms of a concrete species of reality, a particular part of the psycho-physical universe. God is being compared with a parent, a rock and so forth; but it is understood that God is not on the same level as these entities, nor is he really a rock or a parent.[23]

Hartshorne also explains symbolic (or material) predication by contrasting it with literal (or formal) predication. In formal predication no specific entity like parent or rock serves as a basis for comparison. Instead, purely abstract and general philosophical categories such as space, time, becoming, are employed. Thus, symbolic predication since it resorts to specific images is logically in a different class from formal predication which makes use of purely abstract categories, such as necessary, and infinite. Moreover, the alternatives of these categories are restricted whereas symbolic terms like "father" admit of more definite alternatives than "not being a father". Hartshorne explains that not being literally a father opens up all sorts of possibilities having next to nothing in common with one another such as not being alive, conscious, or sentient at all, on the one hand, or being the unsurpassable form of living, conscious creator, on the other. The alternative to being a ruler or sheperd covers a vast number of other possibilities. In contrast, not being necessary is simply being contingent. The same can be said about the other abstract terms, e.g. finite, relative. There is not a variety of possible forms of reality which would constitute an alternative to being relative.[24]

Hartshorne talks of two forms of literal predication: negative and positive.

Negative God-talk uses literal language but denies its applicability to God. When one says that God is in no way corporeal or temporal, one is maintaining that these literal concepts are inadmissible in the case of God. The other type of literal God-talk, in contrast, advances farther by stating that one can speak of God not only literally but positively. Hartshorne is convinced that literal knowledge of the positive kind can be achieved through metaphysics (as defined in the previous section). He has emphatically held this view in the face of much opposition. In his book, LP, he put this on record: "I wish now to emphasize my conviction that the formal predicates of deity are not exclusively negative, and accordingly, some positive properties of deity can be connoted by non-symbolic designations."[25] Much of his time has been devoted to exploring the positive formal characterizations which seem to him compatible with the religious meaning of the term "God". It is Hartshorne's claim that the most completely abstract general terms applicable to God are quite literal and positive. True, there is a *difference in principle* between the way they apply to God and the way they apply to others, but the difference itself can be literally stated. There does not have to be a bluring of the distinction between God and non-divine reality. Hartshorne is thus critical of negative theology for he considers it a mistake to hold, as he believes negative theology does, that no concepts describe God at all. He argues that unless there are definite common aspects between God and creatures, there can be no definite contrasts, either. That is to say, if we do not talk of God literally and positively, we cannot talk of him even negatively for then we would have no point of reference for our negative talk. Moreover, the dogmatic refusal to consider positive formal properties of God results in the impossibility of making even decent symbolic sense out of such religious terms as love or purpose, without covertly abandoning the formal negation. Unless one accepts that some categories apply to God in a literal and positive manner, there is no basis for either negative comparison or for symbolic talk. Both of these ways of talking about God presuppose literal and positive talk. Consequently, Hartshorne stresses that in its own interest, if not in that of religion, philosophy should not lightly renounce the hope of speaking logically and even literally of God.[26] It is positive God-talk that he has in mind.

It seems to Hartshorne that the denial that divine predicates can be both positive and literal comes from a misconception not simply of God but implicitly of the creatures. Our hesitation to speak literally and positively of God is due to the vagueness of the way we describe ourselves. If we have a non-literal, i.e. vague, ambiguous, inconsistent, notion of what creaturely "existence", "dependence", finitude, "relativity" means then we cannot arrive at positive literal ideas of divine "existence", and so on, either. What we should aim at is being literally correct about our understanding of creatures so that we can be so about certain formal positive attributes of God.[27] As we shall see later on, Hartshorne charges classical theism with misunderstanding the nature of creatures as well as of God.

Besides symbolic language and literal predication (both negative and positive), there is a third type of God-talk discussed by Hartshorne. He calls it "analogical". Here one describes God in a way which depends partly upon one's philosophical beliefs.[28] Hartshorne explains that, for instance, God is symbolically ruler, literally necessary, but analogically conscious and loving. We cannot say definitely how divine knowledge or love differs qualitatively from ours although we can express the difference quantitatively: he knows and loves all creatures, we know and love only some. But we cannot have a literal grasp of how God knows and loves creatures for we cannot know and love anything as God does. In this case we have only analogical knowledge of God. The psychological conceptions, then, such as love, will, knowledge, in the context of God-talk are analogical, not literal. They depend to some extent on how we understand them in their human form.

However, Hartshorne also maintains that there is a strange sense in which analogical concepts apply literally to God and analogically to creatures. In comparing creatures with God, we come to an awareness of our defects only in so far as we know the divine standard. We do not first know our defects independently and then, by eliminating them, think of God's perfection. At times we actually use our awareness of God to furnish a criterion for judging man's weaknesses. Our understanding of human knowledge (and the same can be said of the other psychological conceptions) is a derivative one, produced by drastically restricting the idea we have of God's perfection. Given the variety of theories on the nature of human knowledge, Hartshorne is inclined to doubt whether anyone really knows what it is. "Know" in the human case turns out to have a rather indefinite meaning whereas in the divine case one can state simply what God's infallible knowledge means: God has absolutely conclusive evidence concerning all truths. If knowledge is possession of evidence as to the state of affairs, then God simply knows. That is all there is to it, says Hartshorne, whereas no such plain definition will work for human knowledge. Thus, Hartshorne insists that there is room for the belief that we are enabled to learn something about the creatures by our knowledge of the divine.[29]

What we know of God throws light on our endeavours to understand ourselves. But Hartshorne also says, as has been noted earlier, that our knowledge of ourselves, scant though this may be, helps us to grasp God's reality. What the two statements amount to is that our knowledge of God and our knowledge of ourselves complement each other. The correct views of creatures and of God develop together. Our wish to attain clear knowledge about ourselves will bring about a more realistic idea of God and vice-versa. This is why self-knowledge and knowledge of God are apparently inseparable. Neither is clear unless both are somehow clear.

Hartshorne's emphasis on our ability to know something about God, even to the extent of having literal and positive knowledge of the divine through metaphysics, should not mislead us into concluding that Hartshorne means that we can know everything about God. He is equally emphatic in holding that there is mystery about God, not because his essence is inaccessible to us or because metaphysics is impossible, but because ''particular actuality'', even divine actuality is not metaphysical but empirical. Hartshorne makes the distinction between abstract essence and concrete actuality. This is a distinction which will be explained later on. Suffice it to say for the present that what we know of God in metaphysics is, in Hartshorne's opinion, God's essence and not his actuality. God's actuality is beyond the scope of metaphysics and is better known through personal encounter rather than through a metaphysical inquiry. Herein lies much of the mystery of our God-talk. Hartshorne regards the divine actuality as being incomparably more than the divine essence. The latter by itself is an empty abstraction. By philosophical speculation we know only this abstraction, including the abstract requirement *that* the total divine actuality be incomparably, in some sense infinitely, more than any abstraction, any mere attribute. This *more* itself we do not know in metaphysics.[30] He explains further that the metaphysically known God, being abstract, would be God-as-such rather like the world-as-such of metaphysics. Consequently, this God would not be the actual God whom one confronts personally. The God known in metaphysics is not *our* God, i.e. the God with whom we have a personal relationship in religion. It ought to be added, however, that Hartshorne does not maintain that the God of his metaphysics and the God of religion are two entirely different entities. All he means is that there is a difference between knowing God metaphysically and knowing him in a personal encounter as in religion.

As regards our knowledge of God's essence Hartshorne is still cautious. ''Besides all this, even of the mere divine essence no one, I suppose, has yet formulated a theory so clear that its meaningfulness and consistency are put beyond the reach of his doubt, let alone that of others. Questions can be formulated concerning that so far no one has definitely and credibly answered.''[31] Hartshorne's point is that while we can indeed know God through metaphysics and that with its help we should strive to know him more correctly, it should be borne in mind that metaphysics can only give us an inkling of God's essence. It is not in a position to fully explain it. But what Hartshorne is rejecting is the view that as created beings we can know God only as he is not or as he is in the creatures, not as he is in himself. It is vagueness, he tells us, and not blank ignorance that we have to struggle against. He is convinced of the possibility of knowing God's essence because God cannot absolutely conceal himself from *any* creatures. If God is omnipresent, he can never be more than relatively inaccessible. The difficulties encountered in God-talk do not hinder us from having some abstract concepts about God, correct as far as they go.[32]

In spite of Hartshorne's firm belief that his own formulation of the idea of God removes many traditional paradoxes (or contradictions, as he calls them), he is aware that it leaves all sorts of mysteries, some of which are troublesome puzzles to him.[33] He defends his concept of God as being more consistent and adequate to what religion holds; yet he admits that despite the seeming definiteness of certain aspects of his doctrine the indeterminateness and mystery which yet remain are literally infinite. But then this is due to the object of his inquiry. An all-knowing being cannot but remain in some ways unknown to us. Once the nature of this being is taken cognizance of then it will be clear that he will never be as an open book to any man.

In retrospect, we see that Hartshorne definitely claims that metaphysics as he understands it yields literal and positive knowledge of God. This claim is somewhat balanced by his insistence that there is also much mystery surrounding what we do know of God. Hartshorne takes account of symbolic and analogical God-talk as complementing our metaphysical awareness of God. In subsequent chapters, we shall explore what, according to Hartshorne, we do know of God.

NOTES

1. Cf. p. 42.
2. This definition of metaphysics is a paraphrased one. That it is definitely Hartshorne's understanding of metaphysics can be ascertained from his various writings on this subject.
3. A.N. Whitehead, *Process and Reality* (corrected edition, 1978), p. 3 (underlining mine). There are, however, important differences between Hartshorne's and Whitehead's understanding of metaphysics. See, for instance, David R. Griffin, "Hartshorne's Differences from Whitehead", in Lewis S. Ford (ed.), *Two Process Philosophers: Hartshorne's Encounter with Whitehead*, AAR Studies in Religion, No. 5, 1973, pp. 45 – 48.

   Whitehead has been very influential in the development of Hartshorne's metaphysical system. He was for one year Whitehead's assistant at Harvard. He has written extensively on Whitehead's philosophy; some of his articles on Whitehead were republished as WP. On

Whitehead's influence, see, among others, "Interrogations of Charles Hartshorne", pp. 322 – 324. On the other influences on Hartshorne's thinking, cf. "Comment", in Eugene H. Peters, *The Creative Advance* and "A Conversation with Charles Hartshorne at Hiram College". It must be added, however, that Hartshorne is very much an original thinker. He had worked out many of his ideas before coming into contact with Whitehead.

4. CSPM, pp. 20 – 22.
5. Cf. LP, p. 285.
6. *Ibid*.
7. BH, p. 260; also "Can Man Transcend his Animality?", pp. 210 – 211.
8. Cf. CSPM, pp. 159 – 172; also LP, p. 284.
9. "Metaphysics for Positivists", p. 293.
10. "The Modern World and a Modern View of God", p. 76.
11. "Twelve Elements of my Philosophy", p. 10. See also CSPM, chapter 2, and "The Development of my Philosophy", p. 220.
12. BH, p. 268; also "The Structure of Metaphysics: a Criticism of Lazerowitz's Theory", p. 226.
13. Cf. CSPM, p. 20. Hartshorne is aware of the limitations of human knowledge, as he has stated in an early article, "The New Metaphysics and Currect Problems", p. 27. Nevertheless, he is convinced of the possibility of metaphysics as he defines it. He has carried this conviction from the beginning of his intellectual career when he decided to "trust reason". Much depends, he says, on the honesty and competence of metaphysicians, especially in the application of their own method. It may not be an easy task, but it can be done. See, for example, "The Structure of Metaphysics...", p. 232. On disagreements among metaphysicians over their conclusions and Hartshorne's reaction to this situation, see CSPM, p. 168 and BH, p. 277.
14. Hartshorne maintains that this way of checking one's metaphysical conclusions does not involve a circularity of definition. He cites the authority of C.I. Lewis. Cf. "Metaphysics for Positivists", p. 289; also, "Kant's Refutation Still Not Convincing", p. 315.
15. BH, p. 292. It could, of course, be retorted that any statement which claims to fit *any* conceivable experience must be vacuous because what is true of *all* things says nothing about any particular thing. To such an objection, Hartshorne would reply: "Of course, a statement which no observation could count against says nothing contingent about reality. It does not discriminate one possible world state from another. This does not prevent it from being true of any and every such state, hence also (trivially, if you like) of the actual state... It is a strange logical lapse to infer "describes no possible experience" from "conflicts with no possible experience". What could not be false under any circumstances is either nonsense or it is true under any and every circumstance." "The Development of my Philosophy", p. 220.
16. "The New Metaphysics and Current Problems", p. 27. Compare this statement with note 12 and what has been said of Hartshorne's idea of metaphysical statements.
17. MV, p. 34.
18. In his view nearly all the questions that are important for our time are begged or confused by crude or equivocal alternatives. Cf. RSP, p. 17. This is a rather exaggerated observation, but it does show Hartshorne's deep respect for clear and logical thinking. On the role of mathematics in knowledge, he writes: "Mathematics, pure logical form, is almost as important in knowledge as observation. One reason for this is particularly significant for philosophy. The function of observation is not merely to decide for or against some hypothesis but ultimately to decide among possible hypotheses. We do not merely test explanations one at a time against the facts; we bring to the facts a system of possible

explanations to be evaluated against each other. The cogency of the procedure obviously depends, in part, upon whether or not the possibilities for explanation have been exhausted. To be sure of having surveyed all the possibilities, one must arrange them in a formal way, by means of a mathematical diagram, algebraic or geometrical." RSP, p. 20. He has made good use of this method in his philosophical and theological inquiries although he has admitted on more than one occasion that he could have employed logic much more extensively.

19. MV, p. 69; also AW, p. 4 and "The Rationalistic Criterion in Metaphysics", p. 439.
20. "The Development of my Philosophy", p. 215.
21. "Analysis and Cultural Lag in Philosophy", p. 105. That Hartshorne has seriously followed his own advice is confirmed by his extraordinary familiarity with tradition. Cf. Hocking's forword to RSP and Hartshorne's IOGT. Hartshorne calls his philosophy "neo-classical" because it has been thought out in close connection with classical figures. His book (with William Reese) PSG is an investigation into possible ideas of God as found in history. In a letter to this writer, Hartshorne states that he "makes use of history to think clearly".
22. "The Centrality of Reason in Philosophy", p. 5.
23. LP, p. 134.
24. "Tillich and the Non-theological Meaning of Theological Terms", p. 677; "Tillich and the Other Great Tradition", p. 251; "The Idea of God – Literal or Analogical?", p. 134. To present the alternatives as either contingent or not contingent, finite or infinite, is, in Hartshorne's view, to over-simplify. "Not contingent" may mean "necessary" or "impossible" (necessarily false or non-existent). Also, "not finite" can have several meanings as mathematicians know. But all of these are very abstract, unlike being a mother or brother as cases of "not being a father".
25. pp. 134 – 135.
26. "The God of Religion and the God of Philosophy", p. 162.
27. LP, pp. 138 – 139.
28. *Ibid*, p. 134ff.
29. "Are Religious Dogmas Cognitive and Meaningful?", p. 149; also LP, p. 141; "Tillich and the Other Great Tradition", p. 255; "God and Man not Rivals", p. 11. The epistemological basis of Hartshorne's stance is well brought out in the following passage: "Imperfect knowledge, such as ours, seems to imply a non-coincidence of things as known and things as they are, of "reality" and known reality. Yet reality, sofar as simply *not* known, is useless as a standard of knowledge. The standard must be furnished by *internal* characteristics of knowledge, such as consistency, clarity, certainty. The ideal of these qualities gives the definition of "perfect" knowledge. This knowledge does not presuppose "reality" as a standard, hence it can, without circularity, provide a definition of reality." "True Knowledge Defines Reality: What was True in "Idealism"", p. 573. This passage which sets forth Hartshorne's idealism elucidates his reason for saying that we know more of God's reality than our own, inasmuch as God is the ideal.
30. "The Kinds of Theism", p. 129. He also explains this point in NTOT, p. 132.
31. "The Kinds of Theism", p. 130.
32. "Tillich and the Other Great Tradition", p. 255.
33. "Two Forms of Idolatry", p. 13.

PART II

HARTSHORNE'S CONCEPT OF GOD

CHAPTER 3

GOD'S REALITY

In a previous chapter we examined Hartshorne's analysis of the religious idea of God, and took note of the importance he gives to religion as a source of our conception of God. From now on we shall be concerned with his philosophical development of this idea.

In DR he stated that he wants "to formulate the idea of deity so as to preserve, perhaps even increase, its religious value, while yet avoiding the contradictions which seem inseparable from the idea as customarily defined".[1] This statement encapsulates much of what he has set out to do in his writings. By 'religious value" he means "the power to express and enhance reverence or worship on a high ethical and cultural level".[2] The resulting concept of God should be one which an enlightened person would find to be free of logical absurdity and which he could associate with the God he worships. As we have seen, Hartshorne maintains that the God of philosophy should be closely identified with the God of religion and that many of the troublesome aspects of the classical concept of God can be avoided. Hartshorne is keen on a reformulation of the idea of God rather than in defining God himself. Notwithstanding this caution on his part, it ought to be apparent by now, given his understanding of metaphysics, that his attempt to reinterpret "God" is ultimately to describe God as he really is insofar as it is possible. It is for this reason that the distinction between "God" and God cannot be strictly adhered to.

I. God's Perfection

Hartshorne believes that the religious idea of God is best expressed by the phrase "the Worshipful One". However, if God is regarded as the object of our worship — and he is so regarded in religion — then he must be perfect for only someone who is perfect can be admired, respected and reverenced without limit.[3]

God's perfection has been interpreted by classical theism to mean "non-relative or devoid of any relations and therefore incapable of change or increase". It was felt that in order to uphold God's perfection consistently, one must say that he is absolute, completely immutable and totally independent. Hartshorne maintains, on the other hand, that although one can find this insistence on God's unchangeableness in religious teachings, it is God's goodness which is affirmed never to change or "without a shadow of turning". Religion considers God to be all-good; he is completely reliable for, no matter what changes there may be in us, God will not waver in his concern for our well-being. There can be no change whatsoever in God in this sense. Nevertheless, this talk of the constancy of God's goodness does not justify a general conclusion as to God's complete immutability or his absoluteness. To support his view, Hartshorne reminds us that religion also emphasizes God's social and personal nature. For religion God is the highest ruler, judge and benefactor who knows, loves and assists man with a view to sharing his happiness with him. All this would indicate that God stands in a personal relationship to us, a view which leads Hartshorne to question the classical understanding of God's worshipfulness in terms of absolute perfection.

How then should one understand God's worshipfulness so that both his perfection and his social nature would figure? According to Hartshorne, philosophers and theologians in general tended to link up the worshipfulness of God with certain properties such as infinite, eternal, cause of all things, existing necessarily, absolute, independent and so on. By so describing God, they meant to show the radical asymmetry in the relation between God and his worshippers since all of these properties could be appropriately applied only to God. God's perfection on the whole was understood to mean that he could not be capable of any change. Hartshorne, for his part, argues that God's worshipfulness simply means his unsurpassability, rather than his infinity or absoluteness.[4] All that is required for God to be the proper object of worship is that he should not be conceivably surpassable by another.[5] God is "the worshipful one" because he is exalted beyond any actual or possible rivalry; he can be admired, respected or reverenced without limit because he is superior to anyone, now or ever. Thus, he is unsurpassable not only by beings actually in existence but by any conceivable reality. Since this rules out any individual who could theoretically equal or surpass God, rivalry with him is logically and not merely factually excluded. It is this strict logical incomparability of God which constitutes his worshipfulness. Because only God is unsurpassable, he is qualitatively different from everyone else.

Hartshorne's reason for preferring the phrase "unsurpassability by others" when speaking of God's perfection is that this phrase suffices to distinguish the divine reality from non-divine individuals without compromising his social nature. It still puts God in a category of his own. In thus speaking of God's perfection as unsurpassability,[6] Hartshorne is not equating it with immutability or absoluteness but with uniqueness. For God to be worshipful, he must not be conceivably surpassed by another. But he is in all respects unsurpassable only in relation to others. Hartshorne talks of God as being self-surpassable: while God cannot be surpassed by others, he can in some respects surpass himself. While there can be no change whatsoever in God's exalted status, there can be change in God himself. He can surpass himself although not in the sense that he can be more divine but in the sense that he can be affected by what others do.

But surely, if God is worshipful, he must be perfect in himself and not merely in comparison with others. To say that God can surpass himself and change is equivalent to saying that God can grow in perfection. If this is true, then God must not have been perfect in the first place. It was with this counterargument in mind that classical theism chose to regard God's perfection as absolute, i.e. "complete and incapable of enchancement". In its view absolute perfection is the actualization of every potentiality. God as the absolutely perfect being was considered to lack no possible value. God was accordingly described as *"actus purus"*. Because God possesses everything that is in accordance with the nature of a supreme Being, nothing is said to contribute anything to him. God is necessarily all that he is capable of being. Unlike ordinary or imperfect individuals which fail to actualize some of their potentialities, God was conceived to be pure actuality; that is, to have no unactualized aspect of his reality. Classical theism argued that if God did not already possess all possible values, he would not be God.

Hartshorne expresses his objection to this interpretation of God's perfection in the form of an analysis of "perfect". If God, he says, is to be conceived at all and if "perfect" is to be properly attributed to him, then one must ask whether this means "perfect in all ways", "perfect in some ways" or "perfect in no way". This is a formal classification of the word "perfect". Hartshorne uses this method to clarify the meaning of the statement that "God is perfect".[7]

The third alternative "perfect in no way", however, runs counter to the very idea of worshipfulness. Hartshorne, it will be recalled, equates worship with "loving with all one's being". A God who is "perfect in no way" cannot be worshipped, i.e. he cannot be a proper object of worship, since he would be subject to every imperfection and alteration and would therefore be totally unreliable. A God who is "perfect in no way" is imperfect in every way – hardly an object of anyone's total devotion. So the implication of the assertion that God is worshipful, is that God is *not* "perfect in no way". The idea of worship indicates that God, as the term of worship, is perfect, whether in all ways or only in some ways still left open.

As regards the first option, although we tend to equate God's worshipful-

38

ness with absolute perfection ("perfect in all ways") Hartshorne insists that the latter concept does not have a consistent meaning. "Perfect in all ways" is self-contradictory because there are "incompossible values".[8] To hold that God is perfect in all ways is equivalent to saying that God contains all values as actual. But this cannot be, argues Hartshorne, because some values exclude one another. For instance, God cannot know me as writing this *and at the same time* as going for a walk. Both are positive values. If I am writing this now, then God knows me in that state. But in knowing me in that state, God is excluding from the content of his knowledge the other value (my going for a walk). He cannot know me as doing the two things together at the same time since they cannot co-exist. The second value, given the actual existence of the first, is a potential value for me as well as for God. To say that all possible value is actual in God is to make possibility and actuality completely co-extensive and for all purposes identical. This is to eliminate the very meaning of actualization, which is precisely that one does or is this and therefore does *not* do or be that. Since this is what "perfect in all ways" would amount to, Hartshorne asserts that the phrase does not have a consistent meaning and cannot therefore be predicated of God meaningfully.

What remains for our consideration is the phrase "perfect in some ways". But since, as we have already seen, God's worshipfulness means for Hartshorne God's unsurpassability by others, "perfect in some ways" cannot mean that in some ways God will be surpassed by others. It means rather that, while he is in all ways unsurpassable by others, he can surpass himself. He can grow in perfection, he has potential states. (This is in direct contrast to the philosophical doctrine that God is "pure act"). It is this alternative which Hartshorne adopts and develops.

II. God's Relativity

Hartshorne's interpretation of God's perfection as unsurpassability is aimed at doing justice to God's worshipfulness which is the kernel of the religious idea of God. But God's perfection so understood is in some respects relative; and he can, therefore, change. Hartshorne's defense of his position is two-pronged: first, he tries to show the untenability of the alternative positions (that God is in no way perfect, and that God is absolutely perfect) thereby indirectly showing the logic of his standpoint; secondly, and more directly, he tries to demonstrate that his idea of God as relatively perfect comes much closer to religious belief.

As we have seen, Hartshorne talks of the impossibility of maintaining the doctrine of "pure act" due to incompatible values. "There are incompossible values so that the notion of all possible values, fully actualized, is contradictory."[9] One should be careful then about saying that God contains "all value possible" or is "the sum of all perfections" since there are "incompossibles" among possible values; that is, some values exclude one another. While Leibniz, from whom Hartshorne borrows the term "incompossible", had argued that there can be contradiction only between positive and negative predicates, Hartshorne maintains that contradiction exists even between equally positive predicates. "Thus, "red here now" contradicts "green here now". Or if a poet chooses to express a certain sentiment in a sonnet rather than in some other verse form, what is rejected in such a choice is as positive as what is affirmed."[10] The choice is between good or positive alternatives. Actualization, decision, is always exclusive of positive values. Now if the notion of "all possible values actualized" is contradictory, then we cannot affirm it of God. Moreover, if all possible values were already actual in God, there would be no point in our doing anything at all. In Hartshorne's view, there would be no sense in our actualizing possibilities if in the Supreme Being they are actual from the very beginning. As he puts it, "My choices are meaningless if, whatever I choose, the possibilities not chosen can be actual in some other being. Individuality is meaningless and valueless if the very individual value that my personality makes possible, but which I leave unactual, is possible for some other personality."[11] Hartshorne moreover argues that a person selecting a career cuts off from realization opportunities such as could not be thought of in relation to an ape while an ape, at every moment, confronts choices far richer than an amoeba can have. Hartshorne's point here is that the power of selection among partly incompatible possibilities of self-realization seems a measure of excellence rather than of deficiency. It would appear then that "unactualized possibilities increase, rather than decrease, with the rank of a being and that, accordingly, perfection does not mean a zero, but a maximum, of potentiality, of unactualized power to be, as well as to produce beings in others."[12] Divine potentiality for value should be seen as absolutely infinite rather than nil.

Another reason why God has been stipulated as being fully actual and consequently outside all change is the presumption that a being which is capable of change could decrease in value or deteriorate. Hartshorne points out that this belief is a *non sequitur*: the notion of decay or deterioration cannot be inferred from the notion of change. It depends upon what kind of change is involved, or upon how the being is subject to change. Hartshorne elaborates on this argument. "We might as well say that to be able to act well is to be able to act badly; therefore, either God cannot act well or he may act badly. Increase in value is good change, decrease is evil change; the capacity for one does not imply capacity for the other, unless anything good implies the correlative evil.''[13] Although as we ordinarily encounter it, the changeable is corruptible and thus would seem to connote that if God changes, he is corruptible, this argument will be found upon a more rigorous scrutiny to be weak. First, not everything which we ordinarily encounter is applicable to God. Concerning any property or characteristic, the theistic question is always whether it can have a supremely excellent or eminent form unique to God. Since one is talking of eminent change in the context of unsurpassability, one has to rule out the notion of corruptibility.[14] Secondly, if one maintains that God can decrease in value, then God's unsurpassability is nonsensical because another being must be conceivable as superior, namely, an incorruptible being. This would be in conflict with God's unsurpassability.[15] Thus, while ordinary individuals may change by increasing or decreasing in value, God can only increase. He cannot become inferior, even to himself, but he can and endlessly does surpass himself as well as all others. In a word, he is strictly all-surpassing.

Hartshorne claims that God's perfection described as relative has logical validity. He argues that it also enables us to speak of God as truly related to us. Hartshorne's definition of God's perfection leaves open the possibility of taking serious account of a belief in a personal relationship with God, a relatedness that means something not only to us but also to God.

That God is one with whom we are able to enter into a personal relationship is an important feature of the religious idea of God. Nevertheless, if we are to believe Hartshorne, full justice was not done to it in philosophical thinking. The classical interpretation of God's perfection as absolute and consequently devoid of all change makes it impossible to derive any sense from the religious teaching that God loves us. Total immutability cannot be reconciled with the religious stress on God's love and our duty to serve him. Religions teach that what we do makes a difference to God. Because he cares for us, our actions and decisions matter to him. But if all possible values were already actualized in God, then it would be meaningless to do anything at all. There would be no point in serving God. Moreover, if he is unaffected by the acts of his creatures, he is hardly a caring God. Hartshorne takes the statement that "God is love" to mean literally that God shares our joys and our sorrows. God, as the God of love, is one of understanding and sympathy and one to whom we can appeal. He is truly the all-loving and efficacious friend of all. Love, as Hartshorne uses the word even in its application to God, means sympathetic dependence on others.[16] This can only mean, in Hartshorne's way of thinking, that God is really affected by what we do or what we are. In this way we can indeed talk of being related to him and he to us.

On this point, Hartshorne takes Anselm to task for maintaining that God is compassionate in terms of our experience but not so in terms of his own. Anselm's God, according to Hartshorne, does not give us the right to believe that he sympathizes with us. It is a mockery to claim that we feel the effects of God's compassion since the supreme effect of compassion is to give the awareness that someone really and literally responds to our feelings with sympathetic appreciation. Compassion implies that one is *truly*, and not merely apparently, touched by our plight.

Hartshorne anticipates a possible objection, that being affected in response to a situation reveals a certain imperfection in that person, and that it is precisely for this reason that God cannot be said to be affected. His reply is that there is an inappropriate way of responding or of being affected and this is what constitutes an imperfection or a defect, not responding or being affected as such. Hartshorne cites the case of a father and a child. A father who has no regard for the will and welfare of his child is not considered to be an ideal parent. If whatever the child does — be it good or bad — fails to elicit some response from the father, then he cannot be a father who wins our admiration. The ideal in this case is neither that he should remain unmoved nor that he should be swayed by every whim of his child. Rather, the ideal is that the father should be influenced in appropriate, and only in appropriate, ways by the child's desires and fortunes. Likewise, we do not admire a man who is equally happy and serene and joyous regardless of how men and women suffer around him. Nor would it be admirable for him to be dragged down into helpless misery by the sight of suffering in others. Such a response would be equally inappropriate. What is admirable and ideal is appropriateness in one's response, not no response. Applying this to God, Hartshorne says that:

If God is not better satisfied by our good than by our evil acts, and less satisfied by the acts we do perform than he would have been by those better ones we might have achieved, then it is simply meaningless to say that he loves us; and the problem of what the value and purpose of our existence are is without religious answer.[17]

Thus, in showing that God can and does change, Hartshorne wants to give support to the religious doctrine that God is someone personally related to us. In Hartshorne's view, it is essential that we conceive this relationship as involving some change in God.

Hartshorne is persistent in his talk of a certain receptivity or passivity on God's part, arising from God's relatedness to the world. For Hartshorne the

42

notion of divine passivity, elevated in principle above all ordinary forms of passivity, is as intelligible as the notion of divine activity, similarly extrapolated above ordinary forms. He even goes so far as to say that the divine receptivity and divine activity are aspects of one and the same idea. "Passivity *is* activity so far as it is receptive to, or engaged in taking account of the activity of others; and the higher the activity the more comprehensive the receptivity."[18] What marks God out from everyone else is not that there is no receptivity in him but that he alone is affected by everyone and everything. "He can gain from the creatures, but he will be the only one who will gain from every creature, or who will profit from every achievement that others make. Only God could profit from every achievement."[19]

III. God's Absoluteness

So far the stress on God's relativity (God as changing and as related to us) may have given one the impression that Hartshorne's God changes in every respect. But this is not so. God changes, really changes, but not in every respect. In other words, there are aspects in God which do not change. In this sense, he is immutable or absolute. For one, God's superiority is immutable. He remains superior to all others, no matter what. And because he is not only actually but also logically superior, his superiority is one in principle. In this respect, he is a being whose value is a sheer maximum. Secondly, God's capacity to be affected by his creatures does not prevent him from having features which are independent of and unchangeable by the creatures. In this he is completely independent of any given creature. In short, his supreme relativity does not thereby preclude his having aspects which can be deemed absolute or immutable.

God's absoluteness ensures his identity. According to Hartshorne, any changing yet enduring thing has two aspects: the aspect of identity (what is common to the thing in its earlier and later stages) and the aspect of novelty. A being which changes through all time has an identical aspect which is exempt from change. It is in this sense immutable. This is true of God. God was, is, and will always be superior to all others. Nothing and no one can ever challenge this superiority, no matter what happens or what one does. This safeguards God's status. Thus, in spite of what has been affirmed regarding God's relativity, Hartshorne's God retains his self-identity. God possesses an absolutely unchangeable quality, the quality of being universally other-superior, of surpassing absolutely all others.

Inasmuch as God's identity of being unsurpassed by others remains unaltered and unalterable, God is absolute. But God is also absolute in another but related sense; namely, that he is in some respects impassive to the actions of others. No matter what non-divine entities do, they cannot reduce God's status of being superior to all others. Here God is untouchable by them. His identity is radically secure despite what others may do.

It should be borne in mind that what Hartshorne means by God's absoluteness differs from the way it was expressed in the doctrine of *"actus purus"*. The following passage clarifies the difference:

"The absolute" – meaning the unconditionally independent or in every respect non-relative is adverbial, not adjectival. There is or can be no individual thing, act, or person in all respects absolute; but there is a *mode of action* which in all respects is absolute, and the thing or person with this mode of action is God. Each particular divine act is itself, in some respects, relative; for it is an act of self-relating, experiencing, knowing; but if we ask, "How in general does the divine relate itself to things?" the answer is, "Absolutely", i.e. without the slightest lack of transparency. The generic adverb applying to God is thus the long-sought referent of the old term "the absolute".[20]

God's absoluteness is an abstract aspect of his whole nature. God is indeed absolute, but not *the* absolute as though this were his entire character. Since he is more than an abstraction, his absoluteness is only one side of his reality and not the whole of it.

Hartshorne regards God's absoluteness as an abstract aspect of God's reality because God in his philosophy is dipolar: he has an abstract aspect (pole) and a non-abstract aspect which he calls concrete. Neither can be comprehended apart from the other. The abstract aspect of God is what is absolute, immutable and independent while the concrete aspect is what is relative, changing and dependent. The concrete aspect *includes* the abstract and not the other way around. Unless one appreciates this distinction and this asymmetrical relationship between the two poles or aspects, much of what Hartshorne has to say regarding God's relativity and his absoluteness will be difficult to follow.

Perhaps we can shed some light on his distinction by making use of examples. The universe keeps changing, yet we can refer to its changeless activity; namely, the fact that it never ceases to change. We can also speak of a man being the same person as he was twenty years ago even though he has in the meantime changed in many ways. In referring to the changeless activity of the universe or to the man's identity, we are in fact pointing to the abstract element or pole of their realities. In their concreteness, however, the universe and the man change. The concrete realities of the universe and of the man both of which change, include the abstract which does not change. That is to say, the abstract "changeless activity" of the universe does not exist apart from the universe which continuously changes nor is there an "identity" separate from the man who has undergone several changes. The concrete is thus the fullness of their realities. The abstract is something one arrives at by not paying attention to that fullness. The abstract is really a partial feature of concrete reality.[21]

What Hartshorne does is to use the same distinction between the concrete and the abstract when speaking of God. He does not mean a concrete way of talking and an abstract way of talking. He insists that the distinction is ontological: God *is* dipolar, not just our way of referring to him. However, the abstract aspect exists in the concrete; that is, the abstract is real only in the concrete.[22] In the examples given above, the changeless activity of the universe is not real apart from the changing universe; and the man's identity is not separate from the man who changes in many ways. When Hartshorne says therefore that God is dipolar, he has in mind one entity but is taking into account the two aspects of the same entity. Although he is attributing contrasting predicates to the same individual, he is predicating them in diverse ways. When he states that God is immutable and changing, he means that God is immutable as far as his abstract aspect is concerned; he changes as far as his concreteness is the point of reference. Since he is predicating these in different ways, he maintains that there is no contradiction. To quote him on this point: "No rule of logic forbids saying that a thing has a property and also its negative, provided the positive and the negative properties are referred to the thing in diverse aspects".[23]

Hartshorne's way of looking at God's absoluteness as an abstract aspect can be examined further within the context of his discussion on personal self-identity, which in his philosophy is something abstract. "The self-same ego is an abstraction from concrete realities, not itself a fully concrete reality."[24] This is not to say that it is unreal, but it is real within something richer in determination than itself. Hartshorne explains that the "I" spoken by me is distinct from the "I" uttered by someone else because there is a different referent of the pronoun in each case. In the same, though subtler, way the "I" which I say now has a different referent from the "I" which I uttered earlier or which I will pronounce later on. The reason for the difference is that the pronoun "I" (or any of the personal pronouns) is a demonstrative and is context-dependent or token-reflexive; that is, the meaning changes each time it is used. There is, of course, an enduring individuality or a specific subject with definite experiences. But each new experience which the subject undergoes means a new actuality for that subject. The persistent identity itself is abstract while the actual subject having these experiences is concrete.

Thus, there is a new I every moment and the "I" really means not just "I as subject here" but also "I now". In short, spatial and temporal considerations are intrinsic to one's concrete reality. The concreteness of the subject is due to the society or sequence of experiences of which the subject is composed. The referent of "I" is usually some limited part of that sequence of experiences. As Hartshorne puts it, "Personal identity is a partial, not complete identity; it is an abstract aspect of life, not life in its concreteness".[25] This is why it would be erroneous to hold that each of us is always simply the same subject or the same reality even if we must also admit that we are the same individuals. We are identical through life as human individuals, but not so in our concreteness. Concretely, there is a new man or woman each moment. To recognize the sameness of that man or woman, we must disregard that which is new at each moment.

Hartshorne differentiates personal identity from strict identity. Identity in its strict meaning connotes entire sameness, total non-difference, in what is said to be identical. If x is identical with y, then "x" and "y" are two symbols with but one referent. The difference between them is only in the symbols or the act of symbolization, not in the thing symbolized. It follows that x does not have any property which y does not have and vice versa. Personal identity, on the other hand, is literally partial identity and therefore partial non-identity, the non-identity referring to the complete reality while the identity to a mere constituent. Personal identity is the persistence of certain defining characteristics in a very complex reality which constantly changes.[26]

Following this line of thought, Hartshorne talks of God's dipolarity. As was mentioned before, Hartshorne holds that God's abstract aspect exists in his concreteness; that is, the abstract is real only in the concrete.[27] His concreteness is the more inclusive of the two. As mere concepts "abstractness" and "concreteness" are interdependent or symmetrical; they mutually require each other. Hence, there is no inclusion. But when they are regarded as descriptions of concrete things or realities, concreteness is said to incorporate the abstract in that it is the description which tells us what both concepts are about while abstractness describes only an aspect of the concrete, not the concrete reality itself.[28] It is for this reason that Hartshorne repeatedly makes the claim that God is "more" than "the absolute" since this term in his view refers to God's abstractness. God has an absolute aspect, but this is merely a partial description of him.

IV. The Law of Polarity

Hartshorne finds support for the doctrine of divine relativity and absoluteness (or of God's dipolar nature) in the so-called "Law of Polarity". This law expounds further the relationship between the abstract and the concrete.

According to this law, which Hartshorne says he has taken over from Morris Cohen, "ultimate contraries are correlatives, mutually inter-dependent, so that nothing real can be described by the wholly one-sided assertion of [ultimate categories such as] simplicity, being, actuality and the like, each in a "pure" form, devoid and independent of complexity, be-coming, potentiality and related categories".[29] However, although polarities are ultimate, it does not follow that the two poles are in every sense on an equal status. As mere abstract concepts they are indeed correlatives, each requiring the other for its own meaning. But in their application to the reality itself, one pole or category includes its contrary.[30]

This law is said to pervade reality. If one reflects sufficiently, one can expect to find all of reality revealing certain abstract contrasts, such as com-plex-simple, relative-absolute and so forth, which are ultimate or meta-physical contraries. The two poles or contrasts of each set stand or fall to-gether. Neither pole is to be denied or explained away or regarded as "unreal". If either pole is real, the contrast itself (i.e. the two poles together) is also real. Although only one expresses the total reality, its correlative also says something about that reality since it is included in the other pole. There is a basic asymmetry or a one-sided dependence: what is concrete includes what is abstract, but not vice versa. As a result, metaphysical categories as exemplified by concrete realities are always to be found in pairs. No concrete individual is merely simple, it is also complex. There is no such thing as pure effect. The same entity is, in another aspect, also a cause. No concrete entity can be said to be solely necessary for in a different context it is also con-tingent.

This pairing of metaphysical categories runs through Hartshorne's meta-physical system. And inasmuch as God is regarded as the exemplification of metaphysical categories, it is to be expected that he would also be described in dual terms like cause-effect, relative-absolute, contingent-necessary, always understood, of course, as applying to him in an eminent way. As we have observed, Hartshorne does predicate relativity and absoluteness of God.

Hartshorne finds fault with the way some theistic and pantheistic schools violate this principle of polarity by regarding one pole of contraries as superior to its correlative. Consequently, supreme reality cannot be spoken of, according to these schools, in terms of the other and inferior pole. Thus, the phrase "pure actuality" or "the absolute" asserts God be an exception to the law of polarity. In trying to define, analyze and purify the idea of God, these schools of thought tended to take each pair of ultimate categories, such as one and many, permanence and change, being and becoming, then decide in each case which member of the pair is good or admirable and attribute it (in some supremely excellent or transcendent form) to God. At the same time, the opposite term was considered inapplicable to him. The assumption here, Hartshorne wants to point out, is that the highest form of reality is to be indicated by separating or purifying one pole of the ultimate contrasts and rejecting the other pole.[31]

Such a monopolar approach was enshrined in the "*via negativa*" which proceeded by removing predicates as unworthy of application to God. It too uses basic metaphysical or categorial contrasts, e.g. immutable-mutable, but in each case it placed God on the first or negative side of the contrast while putting non-divine realities exclusively on the positive side. This may have been the simplest conceivable way of defining a difference in principle between God and everything else. However, it runs the risk of being inconsistent. Hartshorne has serious doubts as to whether the so-called "superior pole" as interpreted in the "*via negativa*" retains its meaning. He thinks that this approach destroys the alleged analogy rather than gives it the required scope and genuine meaning.[32] For in spite of its doctrine of the insufficiency of human conceptions to describe God, there is in the "*via negativa*" a favoured status for one side of the ultimate conceptual contrasts. This principle of the unequal competence of contrary categories does not follow from the principle of the general incompetence of these categories. Furthermore, in the long run the contrast between ourselves and God is not successfully expressed by putting God on the negative side of metaphysical polarities. The argument that only the negative side of the polarities preserves the disparity between God and us forgets that even negative concepts are still our human concepts. One could also ask how God differs from bare nothing if the meaning of the concepts as applied to God is merely negative.

Hartshorne finds another principle used in classical tradition, the principle of eminence, to be more in line with the law of polarity. Whatever is good in creation is, according to this principle, analogically and eminently the property of God. Thus, knowledge, purpose, life, joy are deficiently present in us, but eminently and analogically in God. In this manner the idea of God acquires positive meaning controllable by analysis and yet free from anthropomorphic crudities. The way of eminence, if consistently executed, treats the categories impartially.[33]

There is a difference, however, between the principle of eminence and the law of polarity. Whereas the first applies categories to God analogically, the second as employed by Hartshorne endeavours to show which categories can be applied to God univocally. In talking of God's knowledge, love and power, Hartshorne makes use of the principle of eminence. But in his description of God's nature, the metaphysical categories are supposed to refer to him literally. Hartshorne's position is that an analogy, to be effective, must be followed by the attempt to spell out where the similarity lies. This is to speak univocally.

The law of polarity in its application to God is known in Hartshorne's philosophy as the "principle of dual transcendence".[34] This principle places God not on one side of the metaphysical contraries but on both sides in uniquely excellent ways, differing in principle from the way in which the non-divine beings are on both sides. The phrase "differing in principle" is intended to show that there is an infinite difference between God and creatures. There is about God a superiority in principle when compared with any other individual. This is because the idea of worship, on which Hartshorne bases his interpretation of God's unsurpassability, is not just an unusually high degree of respect or admiration. The unrivaled status of God cannot be expressed by indefinite descriptions like "immensely good", "very powerful" or even "best" or "most powerful". It has to be clearly demonstrated that God's superiority is one in principle and that there is a definite divergence from every other being, actual or possible. Otherwise, one would be vulnerable to the charge that God is a mere superhuman. Hartshorne calls this divergence "categorical supremacy". It entails that the essential meaning of certain basic concepts must be exhausted if we are truly to regard God as worshipful.

The same law of polarity when applied to creatures or non-divine realities is called the "law of dual immanence". Whatever on either side of the categorial contrast is eminently present in God is non-eminently but positively present in every creature. This is the law of dual transcendence in reverse form. Once again, the dictum that God is the supreme exemplification of, rather than an exception to, the metaphysical categories is being put into operation. For instance, God and creatures are both cause and effect but God is cause and effect in an unsurpassable way while creatures are causes and effects in a surpassable way. The same obtains with the other metaphysical categories. They are true of God in an unsurpassable fashion but are predicated of creatures in a surpassable way.[35]

As has been already pointed out, Hartshorne does not see any contradiction in ascribing opposite metaphysical categories to the same reality provided they refer to different aspects of that reality. We noted how this logic features in the case of the metaphysical categories of relativity and absoluteness: God is relative in his concrete aspect but absolute in his abstract aspect. In Hartshorne's view the law of non-contradiction is incorrectly formulated as "no subject can have the predicates p and not-p at the same time". What needs to be made explicit is that they cannot be applied *in the same respect*. Hartshorne explains that a person can change in some respects without changing in every way and the world may be finite spatially and infinite temporally. Or God can be regarded as immutable in his ultimate purpose but mutable with respect to new specific objectives in response to creatures. He can also be said to exist necessarily so far as his essence is concerned but contingently if what is in question are his inessential qualities. In all of these the predication of contrasting attributes is not on the same ontological level for one set refers to the concrete aspect while the other to the abstract.

Furthermore, it is claimed that the law of polarity does not blur the distinction between God and creatures even if it is valid for both. Any creature, for example, has a temporal beginning and termination, but God has neither. His form of temporality, unlike that of creatures, excludes birth and death; it also rules out corruption or any change consisting in decrease in value, as only increase is possible for him. In addition, God's potentialities are infinite while those of creatures are limited.[36] One could go on showing that God's uniqueness is maintained while stating that every pair of contraries nevertheless applies to God as well as to creatures. Hartshorne sums it up by saying that the uniqueness of God is definitely statable in dual terms.

V. Existence and Actuality

It has been shown that much of Hartshorne's doctrine of a dipolar God[37] revolves around his distinction between the abstract and the concrete. In this section we shall look into how the distinction between existence and actuality is supposed to elucidate further Hartshorne's interpretation of God's reality.

Calling the concrete state of a thing its actuality, Hartshorne says that actuality is always *more* than bare existence. "All existence whatever, including the divine, is the "somehow actualized" status of a nature in a suitable actuality, this actuality being always more determinate than the bare truth *that* the nature exists, i.e. is in some actual state."[38] *That* the defined abstract nature is somehow concretely actualized is what Hartshorne understands by existence. *How* it is actualized, i.e. in what particular state or with what particular content, is what is meant by actuality.

An essence, that is, the abstract definition of something, exists if and only if it is actualized or concretized somehow or is in some concrete form. However, one cannot deduce actuality which is concrete from an essence which is the abstract definition of the thing. In other words, actuality *never* follows from essence. Thus, the essence "humanity" exists if there are men, no matter which men or what states are actualized. But from "humanity" one cannot ascertain which men are actualized.[39] There is a manifest difference between existence (the truth *that* an abstraction is somehow concretely embodied) and actuality (*how* that embodiment occurs).

Since actuality is concrete, it is finite. This means that some possibilities are left out and thus prevented from being actualized. This is because, as we will recall, there are "incompossible values". Actual reality in all cases is limited. Actualization is determination which in turn implies partial negation. It is the acceptance of limitation. It means choosing this and therefore not that. Concrete actuality must always be competitive, it must at all times exclude something else which could be equally concrete.

The distinction between existence and actuality also holds for divine reality. God's existence is quite different from his actuality. God exists necessarily,[40] but his actuality shares the characteristic of any actual reality: finite, contingent, changing, relative and so forth. God will not fail to exist, no matter what happens. But while God is thus free from the danger of extinction, it is something else to say that we do not contribute to the colour and richness of his actuality. That God exists necessarily means that his individual nature is inevitably and invincibly actualized *somehow*, but just how, in what actual states, is a further and contingent truth about him.

God's essence or nature must be actualized somehow in some concrete state or other. But the specific way in which it is actualized cannot be deduced from his essence. What can be derived from his essence, i.e. from a definition of his nature, is his existence. In fact, Hartshorne regards the divine essence as equivalent to the divine existence "because this is the most abstract individual nature there is, and because what is deduced is equally abstract, merely that the most abstract nature is somehow actualized, no matter how".[41]

Comparing the divine reality with ordinary entities with the distinction between existence and actuality in mind, we note two points:
1. All creaturely existence is contingent, but God's existence is necessary. The existence of God is not a possibility competing with other possibilities (competitiveness is the mark of contingency). To say that we might not have existed is to admit that something else might have existed. But nothing can exist instead of God. Hence, his is a non-competitive kind of existence and is, therefore, necessary. This makes his existence radically different from others.

Moreover, that which is contingent is capable not only of failing to exist but of beginning to exist, depending on favourable circumstances or causes. This is not so with God.

2. All actuality, including God's, is contingent. But God's contingency stands apart from ours because unlike us who are contingent throughout in that nothing unique to us is necessary, God's contingent states, in contrast, contain his necessary essence.

We should also take note in passing that Hartshorne's understanding of necessity-contingency is associated with time: that which is necessary is eternal. He argues that possibility and necessity are in the first place onto-logical and only derivatively logical or linguistic and that they are ontological as modes of time or process. "That is necessarily which is always; that happens of necessity which never fails to happen; that exists contingently which exists or happens only at or during a particular or limited time."[42] Time and modality for Hartshorne are not intra-linguistic nor phenomenal matters but ontological. The contrast between the past as wholly fixed and no longer open to decision and the future as partially settled but really open to alternatives is not dependent on language nor on our thoughts. Given the con-trast (which is ontological) between the past and future, what is necessary can be defined as that which has *always* been part of the settled content of the future, and thus has never been and will never be an open possibility.

Hartshorne clarifies further what is involved in the distinction between God's necessary existence and his contingent actuality. In his fixed primordial purpose and basic character, both of which are abstract, God cannot fail to exist. What this means is that his purpose and character must have some appropriate expression and achievement in particular acts and satisfactions, not that his particular acts and satisfactions are necessary. Hartshorne couches this point rather like a challenge: "God must be and must be God, but what if there are alternative possible ways of being God?"[43] God's actuality as expressive of God's concrete reality is intended to take that question into account. God's actuality is contingent: that is, how God exists is dependent on innumerable factors. Any change in these factors will result in a change in God's actuality.[44]

Predicating necessity of God while ignoring contingency – which is what classical theism has done – is actually to do an injustice to God's supremacy. After all, the contingent is also real and hence so is the totality inclusive of the necessary and the contingent. God is that totality, rather than a mere constituent of it. The contingent side of God is the concrete which incorporates the abstract. Hence, God *qua* contingent is more, not less, than God *qua* necessary. Besides, God's contingent actuality includes ours fully and adequately. Any value in us is therefore *ipso facto* in him.[45]

It would appear then that Hartshorne views God as being on both sides of the contrast necessary-contingent in the same way that he regards him as absolute-relative, immutable-changing and so on. The distinction between God's concrete actuality and his abstract existence identifies which aspect is relative, dependent, changing, contingent and which aspect is absolute, independent, unchanging, necessary and so on.

This distinction is also designed to help us appreciate God's infinity. While his actuality, in common with all other actualities, is limited or finite, his existence is infinite in that he has the boundless capacity to be. Any actuality must be somehow finite for actualization is in essence the partial realization of possibilities, not all of which are realizable. But God is the sole being whose capacity to be is absolutely infinite. This capacity is the only strictly unlimited capacity to be. Since potentiality in God's case is indeed infinite, the actualization of God's personality is truly inexhaustible. Concerning God's infinity, one must distinguish between his unlimited capacity to be and unlimited actual being. Hartshorne upholds the first and dismisses the second as a pseudo-concept.

The distinction between God's actuality and his existence together with what has been said about God's infinity discloses what is knowable and unknowable about God. Because God's capacity for actualization is infinite, his actuality remains largely inaccessible to us. This is especially true of his knowledge. All we can declare is that God's supremacy leads to the conclusion that he is all-knowing. But we do not have knowledge of the actual divine knowing of the actual world as this knowledge – when we recognize its nature – is inconceivably vast. Since God's cognitive capacity is perfect, there can be nothing which he is not able to know. Given the unactualized possibilities of a certain world, God is the potential though not the actual knower of these. When they are actualized, God will of course know them perfectly. His capacity to know is infinite. We can imagine that God knows everything since this can be inferred from an analysis of his essence, but we cannot know how or what God does know. In other words, that God knows perfectly is deducible from his essence, but the contents of this perfect knowledge is not. What can in no case be known through mere meanings is not existence or essence (in God the two are identical) but actuality.[46]

In this chapter we saw that Hartshorne interprets God's reality in a different way from the classical understanding of it in that he ascribes to God not only the usual predicates of absoluteness, necessity, infinity, immutability and so on which tradition has associated with the idea of God,[47] but also what has been commonly regarded as creaturely features like finitude, relativity, contingency and so forth. God for Hartshorne is dipolar. He argues that only if God is so conceived can we provide a more consistent and adequate framework for the religious idea of God. The doctrine of God's dipolarity is expressed philosophically by Hartshorne by resorting to the law of polarity, which puts God and creatures on both sides of metaphysical contraries. He also makes use of the distinction between concrete and abstract aspects and between actuality and existence to elaborate on dipolarity. In subsequent chapters we shall explore how this doctrine enables Hartshorne to revise our understanding of God's knowledge, power and love.

NOTES

1. p. 1.
2. *Ibid.*
3. Cf. MV, p. 158.
4. "Divine Absoluteness and Divine Relativity", p. 164; "The Idea of a Worshipful Being", p. 165.
5. "Love and Dual Transcendence", p. 97; also, "Eternity", "Absolute", "God", p. 141; "Twelve Elements of my Philosophy", p. 9.
6. Linguistically, "unsurpassability" is negative. But Hartshorne insists that it can easily be rendered positive by the phrase "surpassing all others", MV pp. 21 – 22, or by "other-surpassing", PSG, pp. 507 – 508. He makes the same point in his examination of the phrase "superior to" which can be understood as "superior to none", "superior to some" or "superior to all others". The third meaning designates the greatest being since a superior or even an equal is impossible or inconceivable. But even "superior to all others" admits of two forms: a *reflexive* case and a *non-reflexive* case. A reflexive case of being superior to all others means that the being in question may surpass itself while remaining superior to everyone else at all times. This is relative perfection. The non-reflexive case of being superior to all others refers to absolute perfection: not only is the being superior in relation to others, but it is inconceivable for it to be in a superior state. Cf. RSP, p. 157. Hartshorne, as has been shown in the text, rejects the second case. He also uses the words "eminence" and "transcendence" to refer to God's relative perfection. Cf. *Ibid*, p. 113; CSPM, p. 227, 231, 236; DR, p. 20.
7. Cf. RSP, pp. 155 – 157 and 182 – 183. Hartshorne also arrives at the same conclusion by analyzing Anselm's definition of a perfect being as "that than which none greater can be conceived" in MV, pp. 6f. and LP, p. 35.
8. Hartshorne's stand that there are "incompossible values" can be copiously footnoted. See, among others, his CSPM, p. 235; "Love and Dual Transcendence", p. 97; "The Dipolar Conception of Deity", p. 280 and AW, p. 32.
9. AW, p. 31. Hartshorne uses the word "incompossible" more often than "incompatible".
10. *Ibid.*, p. 32.
11. RSP, p. 118.
12. LP, p. 37.
13. PSG, p. 509; also MV, p. 113; OTM, pp. 6 – 7.

54

14. "Process and the Nature of God," p. 118.
15. PSG, p. 509; RSP, p. 119; NTOT, p. 127.
16. DR, p. 48.
17. "Philosophy and Orthodoxy", p. 295; "Equality, Freedom and the Insufficiency of Empiricism", p. 23; NTOT, p. 134.
18. "A Philosopher's Assessment of Christianity", p. 169.
19. "God and the Social Structure of Reality", p. 26.
20. "Religion in Process Philosophy", p. 254.
21. "Interview", p. 5. Abstract qualities omit the living process of growth. Thus, an abstraction as such cannot grow or decline, but is fixed regardless of what happens.
22. "Absolute Objects and Relative Subjects: a Reply", p. 175. In AW, p. 23, he reiterates this position but adds that the "two aspects are not on the same ontological level" for one is abstract and the other is concrete.
23. CSPM, p. 233. Chapters VI and XI deal with this topic at length.
24. "The Development of Process Philosophy", p. 56.
25. "Beyond Enlightened Self-Interest", p. 302.
26. "Strict and Genetic Identity: an Illustration of the Relations of Logic to Metaphysics", p. 242; "Personal Identity from A to Z", p. 212.
27. AW, p. 23.
28. "Duality versus Dualism and Monism", p. 52.
29. PSG, p. 2.
30. CSPM, p. 99.
31. PSG, pp. 1 – 2.
32. "Love and Dual Transcendence", p. 96.
33. Cf. DR, pp. 77 – 78.
34. Hartshorne writes that this phrase "principle of dual transcendence" came to him recently.
35. It is outside the scope of this work to illustrate how all of the metaphysical categories can be said to be applicable to creatures. However, some of them (e.g. cause-effect, necessity-contingency) will be dealt with.
36. Hartshorne adds: "Not only are God's potentialities infinite, but God's actuality is, I think (and see no way to interpret Whitehead or my scheme otherwise), infinite in actualities already created. His ultimate divine past is an actual *infinity*, though not the absolute infinity of pure possibility; for it is definite, as the latter is not, and excludes some possibilities for all subsequent actualization." "Letter to author".
37. Hartshorne briefly gives the background to his doctrine of a dipolar God in "Philosophy After Fifty Years", p. 142. He also refers to it in other works.
38. "Tillich and the Other Great Tradition", p. 258. One of the differences between Hartshorne and Whitehead is in their interpretation of God's actuality. Whitehead holds that God is *an* actual entity while Hartshorne regards him as a personally-ordered society of actual entities. See, for example, "The Development of My Philosophy", p. 223.
39. "How Some Speak and Yet Do not Speak of God", p. 276. Hartshorne, however, holds that while actuality can never be deduced even in the divine case, bare existence, the "somehow realized", does follow from God's essence. For this reason he sees some value in the ontological argument.
40. God's necessary existence is being discussed here as a description of God's reality, not as a proof.
41. "What did Anselm Discover?", p. 218.
42. CSPM, p. 100.

43. "Efficient Causality in Aristotle and St. Thomas", p. 31.
44. This point will be explained in more detail in later chapters. But to anticipate that discussion, a quotation from Hartshorne will indicate that it is mainly in God's knowledge that change takes place. This reflects a certain theory of knowledge: "Granting for the moment that the divine existence is necessary, there must also be factual truths about God; and that which in God "makes" them true can only be contingent. Thus, "God knows that elephants exist" cannot be necessary, since it entails "elephants exist" which is not necessary. Hence God's knowledge of the existence of elephants can only be something non-necessary, a contingent or factual qualification of the divine." "The Structure of Metaphysics...", pp. 229–230.
45. "Outline of a Philosophy of Nature, Part II", p. 385.
46. In chapter 2 reference was made to the mystery inherent in our knowledge of God. In the light of the discussion on God's actuality, it can now be shown why, in spite of Hartshorne's insistence on literal positive knowledge of God, he can also claim that God remains mysterious.
47. According to Hartshorne, even the attribute of "simple" can be applied to God so long as this is seen to refer to his abstract aspect.

CHAPTER 4

GOD'S KNOWLEDGE

I. The Divine Attributes

In his restatement of God's attributes, Hartshorne makes distinctive use of his doctrine of God's dipolarity. He maintains that God's knowledge, power and love admit of an abstract as well as a concrete dimension. In their concrete forms they cannot be defined by merely analyzing what is entailed by God's unsurpassable nature since in their concreteness they are manifestations of God's actuality which remains hidden from us. As concrete actualities they cannot be absolutized, either. However, if one were to formulate God's power, knowledge and love in their abstractness, then one can arrive at a definition of their perfect forms. With all three attributes this can be accomplished inasmuch as they can be stated without having to take into account any definite actuality. In this case they would be a type of relation which is definable regardless of how many or which possibilities are actual. This relation can be maximized irrespective of who or what the object may be. For instance, God's knowledge can be conceived of as a sheerly maximal type of response to the *de facto* concrete totality. This signifies that whatever the object of God's knowing is, God will know it fully. Unsurpassable knowledge is clear, certain and adequate knowledge, whose content is all that is, as it is, the actual as actual (without naming what it is), the possible as possible. It is a different matter, however, if we consider God's concrete cognitive response because this depends on the object of his knowledge. Hence, there is no absolute form. While God's knowledge, defined as omniscience, is the best possible way of knowing, the total or concrete shape of this response is contingent upon the particular thing to which he is cognitively related. Since not all possibilities can be actualized, God's concrete knowledge cannot be thought of in maximal terms. Or to put it in another way, God's knowledge is optimal or unsurpassable in freedom from error and ignorance, and in qualitative adequacy, but its aesthetic richness is surpassable, though only by God.

In similar fashion Hartshorne has recourse to dipolarity in his reconception of God's righteousness and power. When he says that God cannot be excelled in his goodness and power, he understands these to have been abstracted from the specific relations which God has toward a particular object or thing and defined without reference to any determinate fact or to any actual object. Thus, ultimate goodness (i.e. goodness taken in its ultimate or unsurpassable form) is regarded as the adequate taking into account of all actual and possible realities, no matter what, each given its due. Ultimate power is defined as power adequate to control the universe in the best possible way.

But as abstract attributes, they must somehow be actualized in concrete form. How and in what form or forms is a contingent matter. Admittedly, God is more knowing, more benevolent, more powerful than any other conceivable being; hence, there is a difference in principle between any divine attribute and the corresponding property in creatures. As an omniscient knower he cannot increase in knowledge if by this is meant overcoming previous error or ignorance. As holy or entirely righteous, God is never guilty of selfishness or meanness. Because he is all-powerful, he cannot be accused of being weak at any time. Nevertheless, all this leaves ample room for and even requires a relative aspect in the concrete forms of these attributes. For the things that God knows to exist and deals with righteously, wisely and powerfully as *existent* are not all the things that *can* exist. God's knowledge, power and goodness, in other words, have also concrete forms. And in their concreteness they share the characteristics of any other concrete actuality.

The concreteness of God's attributes is especially demonstrated in his happiness since one cannot postulate God's happiness to be ever absolute or ultimate. Happiness does not have a merely abstract form.[1] It is a concrete value of experience, unintelligible apart from the actual object of satisfaction. Consequently, no maximum can be consistently formulated for this value. Moreover, God's unsurpassable knowledge would mean being aware of vast misery and intense suffering in the world as well as much joy and immense quantities of pleasure. Absolute happiness could not come from nor even co-exist with a knowledge of the reality of good and evil. A further reason for denying absolute happiness stems from Hartshorne's rejection of the belief that God knows as actual – and therefore enjoys – all the possible beautiful and satisfying objects. To say that possible objects could be just as satisfying if left unactualized is to imply that actualization is superfluous.

II. Knowledge

The rest of this chapter will be an exposition of Hartshorne's reformulation of God's knowledge. But first, how does Hartshorne envisage knowledge or the knowing process? According to him, to know is to relate. The knowing process is a relationship which unites the knower and the known. The two become related to each other though in distinctive ways. The knower (or the mind) is internally related to the object whereas the object is externally related to the knower. In the process of knowing, the mind has the cognitive relation and is receptive of the presence or the activity of the object. In being internally related to the object the mind is open to its influence. The mind is as remarkable for its capacity to be moved by others as for its selfmotion. Memory, which is a mental activity illustrative of the mind's receptivity, is a mode of being influenced, not of influencing. It is the objects which condition the knower, not vice versa. There is an asymmetry involved in the knowing process between the knower and the known for it is only the knower who undergoes a change while the known reality remains independent of that change. Hartshorne himself sums it up: "to know is to receive influence. To be known is to exert influence".[2]

Hartshorne disputes the view that relations can be external to *all* their terms. At least one term he believes, is internally affected. In the case of knowledge, the knower is related in an internal way to the object and is modified by it. Hartshorne argues that if no term is said to be constituted by the relation, then the relatedness is additional to all the terms and must be related to them by a further relation. This could go on indefinitely. Accordingly, he interprets knowledge to be an internal relation as far as the knowing subject is concerned.

But the object of knowledge remains external. It enjoys independence from the knowing process. This is what he means by its being "externally related" to the mind which knows it. The mind is linked to something which is not dependent upon it. Inherent in the nature of knowledge, therefore, is that the knower does not determine but accepts its object. What the knower determines is his response to objects, not the objects themselves. The objects must already be determinate; otherwise, there is nothing to know.[3] Their determinateness is independent of the knowing process and exists prior to their being known. Hartshorne agrees with Aristotle and Aquinas that there are one-way relations of dependency and that ordinary forms of knowing illustrate them. Because things already exist, we can know them. It is not our knowledge of them that causes their existence. In fact, their prior existence is a condition for our being able to know them. Thus, just as Hartshorne contradicts the view that all relations are external, he also refutes the view that they are all internal. According to him, at least one term (in the knowing process it is the object) remains external to and is independent of the knower. (This is an argument which we shall come across when we consider how Hartshorne expresses God's relations with the world.) Objects are constitutive of the knowing subjects even when the object known is someone else's knowledge of the first subject as in the case of someone knowing that one is known or loved. Objects of knowledge are externally related to the knower or the mind.

Experience, argues Hartshorne, supports the theory that the cognitive relation is genuinely constitutive of the knower rather than of the known. This is more obvious in a relation such as love where the relationship has a more noticeable effect on the lover. The awareness of such a union makes a difference to the lover. To be known or to be loved does not have the significance that the knowledge that one is known or loved has.

III. God's Concrete Knowledge

In line with the above theory of knowledge, Hartshorne maintains that God is related to what he knows since God's knowledge is a form of relation. In knowing us God includes us in himself. We are in God by being objects of his love and knowledge. As has been shown, Hartshorne claims that in the process of knowing the knower does not determine but accepts the objects. This does not mean that we could be what we are without God, but that in his knowledge of us, he is internally affected by us. It should also be added that Hartshorne does not intend to say that God has no power over us despite his allegation that as objects of God's knowledge we influence him. The power of God over us, it will be shown, consists in his being the supreme object of our own awareness of him (which is largely unconscious and hence not knowledge in the fullest sense). God influences us through our awareness of him rather than through his knowledge of us.[4]

In Hartshorne's opinion, his claim that objects of knowledge are in each case independent of the knower is in accord with his statement that all reality depends upon God's knowledge of it. Any apparent inconsistency between the two is resolved by making use of the distinction between an abstraction and its instances. Things do not depend upon any *particular* knowledge of which they are objects, not even God's particular knowledge of them, since God could have known the same things in a different knowledge. Things must indeed be known by God but not in any specific way. Any particular state of knowing or any actual experience suffices. As Hartshorne puts it: "Given an entity E, then the class "knowings of E" cannot remain empty; to say this is not to define any particular member of the class."[5] God's knowledge of things is essential in the sense that any entity must not only be or become known but be adequately known. This entails that just as the class "knowings of E" cannot remain empty, the class "adequate knowings of E" cannot remain empty, either. Only God can have such "knowings" so that the logical sense of this is that everything is known and must be known by God. But God's actual knowing of that particular entity is inessential for he could have known it by a different yet equally adequate state of knowing or experience. Simply put, *that* it is known by God is necessary to it; how he knows it is not.

Hartshorne is critical of the "medieval inversion of cognitive dependency" in the case of God's knowledge. On this point he parts company with Aquinas whom he interprets as holding that cognition implies the reality of the known and the dependency of the knower on the known but as denying that God's knowledge discloses a similar dependence on God's part.[6] It is the weakness of human knowledge, Aquinas maintains, that forces us to conform to the object instead of determining them. Consequently, God is said to constitute objects in knowing them; he does not adapt himself to contingent objects but adjusts them to his own purposes. Hartshorne for his part maintains that God can indeed be said to adjust things to his *abstract or long-run* purposes, but he adds that what actually does the adjusting is not the mere abstract aspect alone, but the whole concrete God who in molding objects which he knows and loves is also shaped by them. There is nothing whatsoever in our experience to furnish the slightest basis for the idea of a knower who as whole or in his concrete aspect would be unqualified by his relation to what he knows.

God's concrete knowledge is like our own in that it is constitutive of him as knower. It has also a contingent aspect; that is, God's actual or concrete knowledge excludes positive possibilities. For instance, "God knows that it rained yesterday" rules out God's knowing a cloudless sky all day yesterday. The two cannot co-exist; hence, it is impossible for God to know both as actual. Supposing something which does not presently exist comes into existence subsequently, e.g. yesterday's possibility of a cloudless sky, then there will be a new item for God to know and deal with as such. That he did not know it before or eternally as actual is not ignorance. God's knowledge of a given object in a given situation is contingent on the actual existence of that object. Otherwise, if that object did not exist yet God knew it as actually in existence, he would be in error. Moreover, in the case of decisions which we make God cannot be said to know them beforehand for they do not exist until *we* have made them. Hartshorne therefore rejects the theory that God knows them from all eternity as this would put the genuineness of our freedom to make those decisions in doubt.

God's concrete knowledge indicates that God's reality is not, as is often claimed, relationless or without accidents. God's knowledge that "it rained yesterday" is an accident of his reality for had it not rained yesterday he would not have had that factual information. God's knowledge would take account of any change in the datum. Had it not rained, but could have rained, God would have known it as a mere possibility, not as an actuality. Since the object of knowledge is contingent, God's knowledge of particulars could have been other than it is. To affirm otherwise would lead to the conclusion that something could have been but did not, yet God knew it as having taken place.[7] Evidently, this would be erroneous.

But could one not say, as some do, that God in knowing his own all-causative essence sees all that can be produced by it? Hartshorne's reply to this question is that knowing a cause adequately is indeed to know its possible results. (i.e. a range of possible results) but not the actual results themselves since these are not yet in existence. Causes, he argues, never define any precise actual results although they determine the scope of possible effects.[8] Thus, God in knowing his eternal essence would know all the possibilities so far as these are eternally implied by that essence. But he would not thereby know them as actual. Hartshorne grants that God's essence makes all things possible and that God's knowledge of this essence will yield knowledge of the possible as possible. But it cannot, without formal contradiction, yield knowledge of the possible *as actual*.

The distinction between God's knowledge of the actual as actual and the possible as possible signifies that God's concrete knowledge is finite. Divine knowledge of actuality is necessarily limited to just those possibilities which are in fact actualized. "God could know the actualization of other possibilities were there such actualization, but since there is not, he does not. This implies some finitude in the divine knowledge."[9] It is also indicative of real change and growth in God's knowledge inasmuch as there is change in the object of his knowledge. To know the actual as actual and the potential as potential is not only to be wholly free from ignorance or error but also to be sure of an increase in content should the potential become actual. If it materializes, then it will be knowable as actual rather than merely potential.

IV. Divine Knowledge and Time

Implicit in the above discussion is a certain idea of time which needs to be made explicit. In this section therefore we shall probe into Hartshorne's understanding of time and its implication for divine knowledge.

Future events for Hartshorne are indeterminate. The details of any future happenings are more or less vague outlines so that in reality they can be classified as "may-or-may-not-be's" by which is meant that they are not totally definite. Thus, the future does not consist entirely of "will-be's". This openness of the future can be inferred from certain intuitive data, one of which is our experience of "future" in contrast to "past". In this contrast the future is intuitively understood as that which is not yet settled and that which is in some measure awaiting our free decision to settle. "The future is the as-yet-uncreated, the partly unsettled or indefinite, that concerning which choices are decisions still to be made, and even now in part are being made."[10] The future is thus understood to lack the full reality or definiteness of the past.

Decision-making exemplifies this contrast between the future and the past. A decision presupposes its predecessors but not its successors. If subsequent happenings were already determined in detail, decision-making would be pointless. Even so-called inevitable events have as yet unsettled, indeterminate details since they hinge partly upon the decisions of various persons, decisions which have still to be made. The future is thus experienced as being comprised less of "will-be's" and more of "may-be's". It is our sphere of choice and action, and its openness or indeterminateness gives significance to effort and deliberation. Genuine decision-making is the settling of the otherwise unsettled.[11]

Thus, it can be seen that in life we deal with the future largely in terms of probabilities, scarcely in terms of absolute inevitabilities and impossibilities. Our ordinary practical predictions are really qualified may or may-nots rather than strictly will-be's or will-not-be's.[12] Although the future can be anticipated, it is never completely predictable. In anticipating it, we do not decide what will happen exactly. Anticipation only narrows down the range of possibility in general (or of what is conceivable in the abstract) to the more particular and probable ones which will be realized at some future date.[13] It is misleading then to refer to future events simply as those which will occur. There is a limited range of real possibilities or open alternatives in the future.

As the future becomes present and then past, these alternatives *will be* replaced step by step with the corresponding determinate actualities. The indeterminateness of the future's open possibilities will be progressively overcome. Thus, it is likewise a misrepresentation of the future to believe that there is nothing determinate about it. There must be *some* determinateness, otherwise there would be chaos. Moreover, its absence would destroy all difference between near and remote future and therefore any idea of temporal order. The nearer the future is to us the more determinate it becomes. The determinateness of the future is due to the will-be's and the will-not-be's. This is why at times the future can be predicted, since there are laws which, being general, can be observed as having occurred in the past yet have application to the future. However, to determine what can be decided we do not really consult the future, but only the past. Suppose a predicted eclipse is what is in question. The prediction and the grounds for it are actually based on the past. It is because there is some pattern in the way nature behaves, a pattern which is discernible from previous occurrences and is expected in the future, that there is some determinateness in the future.

If the future is indeed partly indeterminate, then God knows it as such and not as something fully settled from all eternity. True knowledge, the kind of knowledge attributed to God, means apprehending the future in this way. When these may-be's are no longer may-be's but definite actualities, they would be known accordingly. For this reason Hartshorne regards the doctrine of timeless omniscience, i.e. that God eternally knows everything, as being based on the wrong assumption that time is something completed instead of ever-increasing. In his view this assumption denies all that we know of the nature of time. Time, he points out, unites determinate, actual past reality with indeterminate, potential future reality. This union is constantly being enriched by the addition of actualized possibilities so that there can be no ultimate totality for anyone to know.[14] It is contradictory to hold that God eternally knows a future event since what is not eternally actualized cannot be eternally known as actual. The future is genuinely open and this is how divine knowledge apprehends it.[15] God will know definite events only in so far as there are any. Hartshorne asks how God could have known us from all eternity when we had not yet existed so as to be objects of his knowledge. Future events are for God as well as for us really future, i.e. awaiting their full definition and reality.

It could of course be due to our ignorance that the future appears indeterminate and nebulous, but Hartshorne tends to think that in part at least this is the real characteristic of the future. "Our imperfection in knowledge of the future lies," he says, "not in its leaving details unspecified, but in failure to exhibit clearly how far and in what respects the future is determinate and how far indeterminate."[16] Ideal knowledge, on the other hand, would see with absolute certainty, how far the future is limited in its potentialities while yet free within these limits. But even for ideal knowledge the future would still appear as partly open. God will, of course, know all there is to to know; but God's knowledge of the world will grow as the world to be known grows. There is no total creation for him to know in one finally complete act of knowing since the world is constantly enriched by the many acts of freedom which occur in the world. Emerging reality enhances the divine knowledge.

Throughout the preceding discussion there was no admission on Hartshorne's part that God is ever ignorant. He will never have been ignorant of anything that really existed as he will cognitively possess every actuality from the moment of its actualization. Ignorance is the failure to know some existent thing as existent or some possible thing as possible or some partly determinate and partly indeterminate thing as both determinate and indeterminate to just the extent that it really is so. In other words, ignorance is a lack of correspondence between the knower and what is known, a lack of adequacy to the object. Knowledge of what is to happen would be false knowledge if there is in fact no such definite occurrence. If the future is truly unsettled or indeterminate, it would not be ignorance but true knowledge to know it as such. Hartshorne therefore insists that while God knows more at any one moment than at the preceding moment, this does not attribute ignorance to God since there are no actual events to be known prior to their occurrence.

While the future is described as in part open, the past is regarded as definitely closed. Once something has taken place, it cannot be undone. It continues to exist as well. Hartshorne firmly holds that events do not cease to have status just because they are over. On the contrary, they become past by becoming constituents of the events whose past they constitute. Nothing ceases to be once it has been actualized; instead, it becomes included in a new actuality. Pastness thus is not unreality since past events become part of the total reality. Hartshorne illustrates this point by citing a past event, Washington's crossing of the Delaware. Since this crossing is now over, one will not find Washington going across this river. Presuming that there really had been such an event, then it is true that Washington made that crossing. But the fact that it is over does not make it non-existent. There cannot be a truth about nothing — which would be the case if we say that that event no longer exists. Hartshorne argues that the crossing does exist and exists on the Delaware so far as space is concerned but in the past part of time. This existence in the past is nevertheless somehow true today and true for all future time. It can never be true that the Delaware was uncrossed by Washington. Time does not destroy anything that occurred nor can it turn a happening into an unhappening.

It would appear then that the past is indestructible. If the past were nothing at all, then propositions about it would be empty for they would have no referents. The truth about x is impossible without x; if x had been obliterated, it would be meaningless to refer to it. As Hartshorne puts it: "Truth is a relational function; if a proposition about x is true, its truth consists in the relation between itself and x, if x is nothing at all, then so is the relation of which it is said to be a term''.[17] Does Hartshorne then deny destruction? The answer here is a qualified one. Event or occurrences cannot be annihilated; things, however, can be. But the annihilation of things consists not in the destruction or removal from reality of the events forming their histories up to the moment of destruction but only in the prevention of additional events belonging to this history. That is, no more such events will be created. Hartshorne explains that men and trees and cities can be destroyed. But what this really means is that an event sequence with a certain persistence of character and with peculiarly intimate relationships among the member-events may have a final member. Or to use Hartshorne's metaphor, the book itself is not destroyed just because the number of chapters has been limited due to the appearance of a last chapter. Neither is a life, properly seen as an event-sequence, turned into naught by virtue of the limited number of its experiences and behavioral occurrences.[18] In short, the past does not consist of unrealities or of nothing but of the very events which have happened.

The past continues in existence by being preserved in the present. This is exemplified by memory since it is in our memory that we know and retain the past. For Hartshorne memory is one way we experience the past as real in the present.[19] But our memory is so feeble that the events we remember are not fully preserved for us by the fact that we remember them. Yet the events we best remember are the ones most nearly preserved as real. For instance, we can remember a certain wonderful moment so well that the beauty of it is almost fully embodied in the present by that memory.

For the past to be fully preserved, there must be a perfect memory such as divine memory. The past is contained in the present to the extent that it is retained absolutely in God. God's perfect knowledge means that all the past must still be before him without loss of any detail or quality. From this memory neither joy nor pain once experienced anywhere in the world can ever be wiped out. Thus, support for the doctrine of the total indestructibility of the past is found in the supposition that there exists a divine memory. Since human memory, whether individual or collective, cannot contain all that has happened and since the past must be regarded as nevertheless real, Hartshorne turns to a memory which, by definition, meets the need to preserve all events. Experience shows that the past is deficiently continued in human memory, and yet the very notion of truth seems to demand the persistence of past events in all their details about which there is truth. The only possible reconciliation of those two statements is to posit a memory that is able to perpetuate the past completely. One senses the existence of such a memory – a memory which is perfectly conscious, clear, vivid and retentive – by contrasting it with one's own imperfect memory. Such a model memory would possess the whole quality of the past, all its joys and sorrows, contrast, harmony and discord.

If what Hartshorne says about God's memory as preserving fully all past events is taken in conjunction with what he has stated as regards the constituting characteristic of knowledge, then the question of how evil affects God arises. The problem of evil will be dealt with in more detail in a later chapter, but some passing comments are in place here. Hartshorne maintains that evil is also in God in that God suffers evil acts and that he is a being to whom suffering is never alien. God knows evil, remembers it for all time and is affected by it. God contains evil, but is not evil. Hartshorne clarifies the significance of this distinction through an analogy. A house, he says, can contain small bricks and yet not be small. A knowing subject may know an erroneous belief that someone else holds or a wicked deed that someone else has committed. His knowledge does not make him guilty of error or of evil since the belief and the deed are not his even if he possesses them as data of knowledge. Analogously, God as perfect knower is totally aware of evil and is affected by it; but he cannot himself be described as evil.

Furthermore, the claim that God includes evil in himself through knowledge does not mean that there is any danger of disvalue overbalancing value. In Hartshorne's view every concrete experience *as a whole* is a value rather than a disvalue. Although God's ability to retain past evil as well as good means that the most terrible happenings would be preserved along with the best ones, Hartshorne still believes that there is more good than evil in life. There is a balance of good over evil which results in the perpetuation of more good than evil. This truth frequently escapes our notice; hence, we sometimes wish to forget what has taken place because we are unaware of all the good that has occurred simultaneously as the evil we wish to forget.[20] Thus, the complete retention of the past in God's memory really means that ultimately value or good will still override whatever disvalue or evil there is.

The past is not and cannot be cancelled out. It is indestructible. This argument is sustained by the claim that the past is in God without loss of any detail or quality. The past then being imperishable, Hartshorne describes our relation to it as that of a spectator: we can do nothing about the past, it has been what it has been, and no power can alter the fact that it has been so.[21]

V. Omniscience and Infallibility

Up to now we have been dealing with God's concrete knowledge as finite, relative and changing. Notwithstanding this description of God's knowledge,

God as knower is held to be omniscient and infallible. This is because Hartshorne understands omniscience and infallibility to be abstract, i.e. they can be defined without reference to any particular fact or datum. Omniscience and infallibility are not determinate actualities but properties or attributes which characterize God's knowledge. They are the common denominators of all possible divine states of knowing. They guarantee that without fail there will be knowledge in God appropriate to him. Being omniscient, God knows everything there is to know; being infallible, his knowledge is as adequate as possible to the object known. He knows and will know as actual whatever is actual and as potential whatever is potential and in as adequate a fashion as possible. Infallibility and omniscience mean clear, certain, adequate knowledge whose content is all that is *as* it is.

Hartshorne argues that this interpretation is consistent with the fact of change.[22] It asserts that whatever happens in the world, God knows it in an omniscient and infallible manner. But it also takes into account that to know infallibly and fully that A exists is a different state of cognitive actuality from knowing infallibly and fully that B exists instead. God's knowledge is said to have an abstract aspect which admits of an absolute maximum in that it is completely free from error and ignorance. But just as God is not adequately defined by referring only to his absoluteness so the abstract perfection of knowledge, its freedom from error and ignorance, is not the entirety of God's knowledge as this depends also upon the richness, diversity and harmony of the reality which is known. God's knowledge of particular objects is modified by them. Hence, the concrete reality of the divine knowing is relative to the object of his knowing and takes on its features, but the abstract perfection which is the necessary and eternal prerogative of God's way of knowing is untouched by the object.

The statements "God is all-knowing" and "God knows that it is raining now" thus belong to two different classes. The first merely defines what a supreme knower is whereas the second tells us some of the content of his knowledge. Moreover, the referent of the word "God" in the two cases is different. The second, but not the first, refers to God as possessing a certain contingent predicate inasmuch as it may not be raining. In that case God would not know it as a present occurrence. Nevertheless, he would still have been all-knowing. God is necessarily an omniscient being and the statement "God is all-knowing" is a necessary one. In contrast, God as the knower of a specific event is contingent, and the statement "God knows that it is raining now" is also contingent. The referent of this statement is God as concrete.

God's knowledge is not just another case of knowing; omniscience and infallibility are properties which nothing else in the world can exemplify.

Divine knowledge is radically different from ours and surpasses ours not merely as ours surpasses that of the animals. God's knowledge is, as Hartshorne expresses it, *the* standard or norm. God is the measure of truth since God and he alone is able to establish a perfect correspondence between his knowing and what he knows. In fact, the phrase "all things" simply means "whatever God knows".[23]

When we compare human knowledge with divine knowledge, we discover that human knowledge is fallible and incomplete. However, it is not the relativity of human knowledge that makes it fall short of the divine. Instead, the fallibility and incompleteness of our knowledge consists in the drastically restricted scope of certain aspects of the relativity of our knowledge. God's knowledge, by comparison, is unrestricted in its relativity. The deficiency of our knowledge lies in being neither exactly relative to the world to be known nor wholly independent of this world but something in between. Moreover, the relativity of our knowledge differs from God's in intensity. Relatedness, Hartshorne says, admits intensive and not just numerical or extensive gradations of clarity as well as of scope. God's act of knowing relates him to the object of his knowledge with such clarity that our own cognitive relatedness is almost equivalent to non-relationship. Compared to God's, therefore, our knowledge is not merely finite and restricted but also fallible, fragmentary, partial, and uncertain. In all basic respects it can be outdone by others more clever and more fortunate than we are. God's knowledge, on the other hand, is always complete. This is because it covers the whole of reality with certainty and ideal clarity. Between God's knowledge and ours there is thus a difference in principle.

Another feature which underscores God's uniqueness as knower is that God's knowledge is infinite in a definite and unmatched sense inasmuch as the totality of possible world states is infinite. Not only does God know this infinite totality, but he could and would know the realization of any of the possibilities were it to be realized. Thus, his potential knowledge is absolutely infinite in the strictest sense. Nothing could exist without his knowledge. While creatures are limited not only in their actual but also in their potential knowledge, God's capacity to know has no limitations.

This chapter pursued Hartshorne's doctrine of God's dipolarity in its application to our understanding of God's knowledge. Hartshorne is far from denying that God is omniscient and infallible but is insistent that to uphold God's superiority as a knower, one does not have to reject the relativity of his knowledge so long as this is taken as referring to his concrete knowledge. In turn, admitting relativity, finitude and contingency (and all characteristics of concrete knowledge) in God's own concrete knowledge does not put it in the same category or class as non-divine knowledge. There is a real divergence between the two.

NOTES

1. Hartshorne explains: "Happiness does, I rather think, have an abstract form, a kind of adequacy, though I may not have said so. God derives, as much beauty in experiencing the world as possible, and the divine aesthetic enjoyment is the only one that covers the *de facto* whole and makes the most of it. This is not the best possible enjoyment of that whole, for a "best possible" divine action would be the only possible divine action. Possibility is too indefinite to be dealt with as Leibniz did. "As good as possible" is all one can say. "Optimal" might be defined in this way, but I am not sure that anyone has said so. "Letter to author".

2. AW, p. 29.

3. "Divine Absoluteness and Divine Relativity", p. 165; also CSPM, p. 12.

4. Hartshorne explains that "God as influencing me *now* is God as knowing me as I have been, not as I am now, God as knowing me as I am now will not influence *that* state of me". *Ibid.*; cf. also PSG, pp. 513 – 14; "Idealism and Our Experience of Nature", p. 79. This point will be explained further, *Infra*, pp. 79

5. "Absolute Objects and Relative Subjects", p. 180.

6. He discusses what he considers to be the reasons for this inversion and his criticism of these reasons. Cf. AW, pp. 10f.; DR, pp. 6f. According to Hartshorne, his explanation presupposes a theory of individuality and personality such as has been discussed in chapter 3. Cf. "Absolute Objects and Relative Subjects", p. 180.

   It has also been suggested that in the case of God's knowledge, it is the thing known which is really related to the knower while for God the relation is "in idea" only. The distinction is therefore made between a logical relation ("in idea") and a real relation. In the knowing process, the mind is regarded as being only logically related to the object because the object itself is not in the knower's mind. Only a representation of it is there. This is what has been referred to in the Thomistic school as a "relation of reason" or a "relation in idea". But Hartshorne insists that if "in idea" means "in God's idea", then his point has been granted. The relation is after all in God. To say that God's relation to the world is "in idea" only is merely to postpone facing the issue: it is either God's idea or it is not. If, on the other hand, it means "in our idea", then it would mean that the world is really related to God, but not vice versa. But this is to incur criticisms which Hartshorne has been bringing up, such as that God cannot be said to really love the world in any convincing way.

   Hartshorne advances the argument that there is nothing whatsoever in all our experience to furnish the slightest evidence that there can be a knower who as whole or in his concrete aspect would be unqualified by his relations to what he knows. He admits that inferential, symbolic, indirect knowledge, "knowledge about" rather than "knowledge by acquaintance", has as its object something relatively external to the knower; but he answers this objection by saying that this knowledge is admittedly and in principle incapable of perfection. Thus, it cannot be the model for understanding God's knowledge. Secondly, even this knowledge conforms the knower to the known, although in a limited, indirect way. Cf. MV, p. 240.

7. PSG, p. 510; also "The Divine Relativity and Absoluteness", p. 149; "Ob Göttliches Wissen um die Weltliche Existenz Notwendig Sein Kann: eine Erwiderung", pp. 469–471.

8. This particular objection stems from Hartshorne's interpretation of causality as creativity, cf. *Infra*, p. 74

9. "The God of Religion and the God of Philosophy", p. 163.

10. "Religion in Process Philosophy", p. 251. In another work Hartshorne writes that "the future does not consist exclusively of what will happen, but also of what within limits may or may not happen, the limits being referents of the *will* and the rest of the *may*". "Necessity", p. 293.

11. This will be dealt with again in the section on creativity.

12. "The Meaning of "Is Going to Be"", p. 53; also "The Reality of the Past, the Unreality of the Future", p. 250; "Duality versus Dualism and Monism", p. 59.

13. RSP, p. 161; "Real Possibility", p. 595f.

14. PSG, p. 11.

15. Hartshorne proposes modifying this doctrine. He formulates the famous Boethian definition of the divine eternity, that it is the *totum simul* or the vision of all things in a single immutable intuition or spiritual state, as follows: "At each moment, there is a divine intuition of all past events. This intuition is single or unitary, so far as that totality, that "all", of events is concerned. However, the next moment there is partly new totality, since additional events have occurred; and this new totality is then embraced in a new *totum simul*. Thus the divine state is ever growing, it acquires additions but suffers no losses. Each item of divine knowledge is immutable, but there is no final totality of items, no final summing up of reality." "Eternity", "Absolute", "God", pp. 131–132.

16. "Ideal Knowledge Defines Reality: What was True in Idealism", p. 575.

17. "The Logical Structure of Givenness", p. 310.

18. "Religion in Process Philosophy", p. 251.

19. RSP, p. 160. Once again we can see in this argument Hartshorne's apparent disregard of the distinction between a logical entity (in this case, the event as remembered) and real entity (the event itself as it is happening). For Hartshorne the event and the event as remembered are placed on a similar status. However, he holds that the past fully present is present not in the temporal sense but in the epistemic sense. The past is said to be present epistemically, otherwise it would be unknowable. Cf. "Eternity", "Absolute", "God", p. 133.

20. "The Reality of the Past, the Unreality of the Future", p. 249; see also, "The Immortality of the Past...", p. 102.

21. RSP, p. 161. No reference was made here to Hartshorne's stand on God's knowledge of the present. This is because in his more recent philosophy, he has defended the view that the present is really the past. He has rejected his earlier stand on simultaneous symmetrical interaction between contemporaries. This shift in his thinking is mentioned by him in a number of writings. See, for instance, "Interrogations of Charles Hartshorne", p. 324; CSPM, p. 122f.; "Interview with Charles Hartshorne", pp. 7–8.

Two interesting articles recording this change in Hartshorne's position and its consequences have been written by David R. Griffin, "Hartshorne's Differences from Whitehead", and by Frederic F. Fost, "Relativity Theory and Hartshorne's Dipolar Theism", in Lewis S. Ford (ed.), *Two Process Philosophers*. But it does not mean that Hartshorne takes the distinction between past and present to be unimportant. What he wishes to state is that the past is not unreal, not that there is no difference between the "already achieved" and the "achieving that is nascent, is coming to be". Past actuality is now immune to an influence, but present actuality is what we are now determining. "Letter to author".

22. In "The Rationalistic Criterion in Metaphysics", p. 440, Hartshorne shows that infallibility has a clear logical meaning. On p. 444 he argues that it is consistent with change.
23. "Ideal Knowledge Defines Reality: What was True in Idealism", p. 577. Hartshorne does not mean that the objects of his knowledge are *mere* ideas.

CHAPTER 5

GOD'S POWER

Hartshorne's reformulation of the way we should speak of God's power is probably best discussed in the context of "creativity", a metaphysical description of the workings of reality. Creativity is a fundamental idea in Hartshorne's metaphysics. The importance that he gives to this category can be appreciated from the fact that he has felt it necessary to start CSPM (which he regards as the nearly definitive statement of his metaphysical position) with a discussion of this idea.[1] It is put forward here not necessarily as a valid interpretation of reality but as an aid to understanding Hartshorne's position vis-à-vis God's power.

I. Creativity

Creativity is an attempt to communicate the significance of existence. Hartshorne also uses the phrase "creative synthesis" to describe this insight into reality. The phrase is well chosen as it brings out the novelty (creative) and partial determinateness (synthesis) of each act of existing which results in an experience. In every experience there is an element which is new as well as an element which is old.

The old consists of the previous experiences which gave rise to and which persist in the new experience. In a single momentary experience one can detect a diversity of data or things experienced: the prior products which entered as data or elements. Thus, there is a great deal of permanence for in the synthesis the data are preserved, the synthesis being the holding together of the data. Experiencing is thus a perpetual unification of a pluralistic reality which, as fast as it gets unified, becomes pluralistic again and so can never be finally unified. The many become one which in turn produces a new many and so on. In other words, there is a synthesis of previous acts or experiences. It is an accumulation of these prior acts or a "putting together" of factors into a whole. Each synthesis is a single reality, not reducible to the interrelated parts yet including those parts. It is a "whole of parts" for it is an inclusive reality and the parts are the included realities.

The novel or creative feature of each act is in the unification which effects a different entity. It is novel because a different kind of experience has emerged from the coming together of past experiences. Previously there was the separate existence of the included realities. Now there is a unity. The synthesis is spontaneous or free because none of these experiences – individually or collectively – dictated the exact unity that would arise.[2]

The descriptive term "creative" suggests that the resulting synthesis was not wholly contained in or strictly implied or entailed by the previous data.[3] The creative aspect of a particular experience lies in that it is never literally anticipated. Initial conditions or causes always restrict the possible outcome, but they never specify it with absolute precision. This lack of precision is not due to our ignorance but rather to the very meaning of creativity. As Hartshorne puts it, "To ask "why may not the antecedent cases completely determine the given?" is to show that one has not grasped the meaning and pervasiveness of creativity or spontaneity."[4] There is a certain originality or freshness in every experience. Inasmuch as it is creative, it is unpredictable, undetermined in advance. A synthesis *emerges* rather than is determined. This is why an experience cannot be fully described in its total unitary quality merely by specifying what its constituents are. Each experience enriches the totality of reality by an additional member.

Creativity is a metaphysical category in the sense explained before. It is rooted in experience although in itself it is not empirical. Like other metaphysical categories, creativity is universal in that it pervades reality, i.e. every actuality is creative. Everyone and everything actual is a creator; in its own way, creative of one's self (self-creation) and creative of other individually distinct beings. There are, of course, different levels or degrees of creativity, corresponding to the extent of novelty or of not being determined by others. The more creative one is, the more free one is of the limiting influence of others. The less one is determined by various factors or causes, the less chance there is of predicting what is going to happen. Hence, there is a corresponding increase in novelty and spontaneity.

How much creativity there is or to what extent creatures transcend causal conditions is often difficult to specify. Nevertheless, Hartshorne is of the opinion that there is always some form of creativity present in creatures. Its presence can be underestimated as well as exaggerated. For Hartshorne "to be is to create". It is impossible to exist at all in absolutely uncreative fashion, he contends, and all things – from atoms to deity – in their degree and kind act creatively. Every individual creates and could not fail to do so while in existence.

What has become apparent is that Hartshorne's doctrine of creative synthesis (or creativity) is actually his interpretation of causality. Every act is seen by him as creative. But the creative act is influenced by its past acts and does require them even if it cannot be determined precisely or fully by these antecedent acts, which are simply earlier cases of freedom. What gives the new experience partial determinateness are previous experiences. The restrictions to freedom which ensure that it is never absolute, are set by other acts, those of oneself or others, including the divine creativity.[5] Consequently, Hartshorne defines causality as the way in which any given act of creativity is influenced or made possible, but yet not fully determined, by previous acts.[6] Because past free acts narrow down any creative act, there can be a certain measure of prediction. Hartshorne compares the principle of causality to the banks of the river which give the flowing water its direction but do not completely determine its movement. "Causality is the boundary within which resolution of indeterminacies takes place. Causal regularities mean not the absence of open possibilities, but their confinement within limits."[7] These past acts condition the new act; that is, they establish and limit the possibilities for an otherwise free and creative activity. But they never determine them fully.

According to Hartshorne, events must have causes. As effects, events presuppose a cause or causes. In this sense then a cause is necessary; it is a *sine qua non* of an event. But in Hartshorne's version of causality when all the necessary conditions for an event will have been fulfilled, it does not follow that the event will take place in precisely the way it is predicted, merely that it may take place. A cause is necessary, but not *the* effect. There will be *an* effect but not a specific or a fully determined effect.

There are also conditions which are sufficient to bring about an effect, but what suffices for its actualization is only the new act of existing inherent in the present effect and not in any past or eternal cause at all. Hence, Hartshorne is critical of the axiom that "the cause cannot give what it lacks". This appears to him to be saying that temporal genesis is a mere passing out, or passing on, of something already real in the cause. His own position is that it is growth, a passage from less to more; in short, creation. The effect is not given nor does it come from an antecedent haven. Simply put, it *becomes*.

Hartshorne believes that his interpretation of causality is supported by contemporary science. He argues that an increasing number of scientists today regard causal laws as statistical rather than determinate.[8] Many older systems of metaphysics, following the most obvious interpretation of Newtonian science, viewed causal laws as uniquely determining the outcome of every situation. Once adequate understanding of the conditions had been arrived at, the result was considered to be wholly a foregone conclusion. Hartshorne maintains that science has grown more and more critical of this assumption. Quantum mechanics strongly suggests, if not actually proves, that causality is

76

essentially different from the older conception of it. Individual events happen at least in a seemingly random or fortuitous manner within certain limits. Causality is the limitation of this randomness. Only when large numbers of similar events are dealt with can there be a highly exact predictability.[9] A cause is conceived, therefore, as related to its effect not by necessity but by probability. This means that the existence of the cause signifies that there shall be *some one of a class of more or less likely outcomes*. The cause necessitates the occurrence of *some* effect or other with a specified range of variability. "In physics", he writes, "this relation is even convertible, the effect necessitating, not any uniquely specifiable cause, but only a class of causes as variously probable."[10] Although it is untrue to state that literally anything could happen in a given place and time, what happens is never the only thing that could have happened despite the often exceeding narrowness of the range of causally permitted alternatives.

And if one turns to recent philosophy, one will find, Hartshorne tells us, evidence for the view that time is asymmetrical in its logical structure so that while the "earlier" never entails the "later" in its individual details, the "later" does strictly entail the "earlier". A man's childhood is essential to his manhood, but not his manhood to his childhood. Not every child even becomes a man at all, but every man has been a child. The present involves the past at least more completely than it involves the future. Events sum up their predecessors but not their successors. Successors are additions or creations. They are not deducible from nor in any sense whatever contained in the present events.

The interpretation of causality which Hartshorne entertains is therefore the statistical or indeterminate one: what is predictable is never particular events but classes of events. This means that it is not the later happening itself, i.e. the effect, which can be fully anticipated, but the sort of happening, the class of more or less probable happenings of which there must be some instance or other. It is really created in the sense of "creativity".[11]

It should be clear by now that creativity or freedom is enshrined in Hartshorne's interpretation of reality. Consequently, he repudiates absolute determinism. He believes that the ultimate meaning of creation lies in the freedom or self-determination of any experience. This is why an experience arises out of the previous many but cannot be fully described in terms of a strictly causal relationship. Absolute determinism, on the other hand, views a happening as already completely predefined in its antecedent causes, each state of the world described as containing in effect an absolute map, as it were, of all subsequent and all previous states. Absolute determination admits, however, that man perhaps will never be able to read the maps except in radically incomplete and inaccurate ways. But Hartshorne regards this doctrine as an incorrect reading of the universality of causation because it is too strict an interpretation. Hartshorne for his part defends an indeterministic explanation. Thus, in spite of his admission that every event has its cause or causes, he maintains that no event in its concrete actuality is fully and absolutely determined by its causes. Furthermore, he generalizes this principle to include even inanimate objects with the result that he upholds universal creativity.[12]

II. Supreme Power

Traditionally, the notion of omnipotence which was descriptive of God's power was defined as "being able to do whatever is intrinsically possible or self-consistent". Hartshorne believes that this definition can be misleading in that it can be taken to mean that God can do anything that can be done. This would in turn result in a claim that God has a sheer monopoly of power or decision-making, that he makes our decisions in their full detail and concreteness and thus that the only genuine decisions are God's. This is a conclusion that Hartshorne regards not only as suspect (since it makes God out to be tyrannical) but also non-sensical.

He suggests that God's power should be designated as "unsurpassable power over all things" inasmuch as this recasting of the doctrine would merely state that God's power is the maximal degree or kind of power compatible with a real plurality of powers.[13] God's power is absolutely maximal, the greatest possible, but even the greatest possible is still one power among others. It is, in brief, not the only power.

God can do everything that can be done by a being with no conceivable superior.[14] He is able to maintain the world. His is the power, which Hartshorne describes as "adequacy of cosmic power", to do for the cosmos all desirable things that could be done and need be done by one universal or cosmic agent who is unmatched by anyone. In this sense God's power is absolute since it is absolutely adequate. God is depicted by Hartshorne as the being uniquely able to maintain the society of which he is a member, the *only* social being unconditionally able to guarantee the survival of that society. God's power is sufficient to preserve the society or the cosmos, no matter what others may do. But God's power does not entail power to do for the cosmos what could only be accomplished by non-universal agents. Such deeds are really theirs, not God's. This is because God's power although perfect in form is still social. Looked at in this way, it is power to set limits to the freedom of others, but not to destroy it.

In many of his writings Hartshorne stresses that God's power is exercised not over the powerless but over real powers. Power acts upon power. To regard non-divine entities as having no power of their own is to jeopardize their existence as "others". To be is to have some power because it is the actualization of some potentiality. Actualization is to some extent self-creation. A plurality of beings therefore connotes a plurality of powers. In Hartshorne's philosophy which regards creativity as a metaphysical category, every item of reality is creative and thus exercises varying degrees of power; it can to some degree decide what it is to be. Supreme creativity permits and demands a division of creative power.[15] Or as Hartshorne puts it, "The creatures must determine something of their own actions, and to this extent the supreme capacity to influence others cannot be a power unilaterally to determine the details of reality."[16] Realities other than God must have their appropriate, non-eminent forms of creativity. Only God has unsurpassable freedom. Only man has human freedom. But dogs have what Hartshorne calls doggish freedom and atoms atomic freedom. There is, in short, a variety of powers. This variety means that every concrete effect has numerous real causes, among which God is the supreme but not sole cause. Hartshorne is not denying that God is an efficient cause of creatures. In fact, God alone is universally and with ideal efficiency causative, but he is not the only causative agent.

In the past God as supreme cause was judged to be in no way an effect. But in Hartshorne's view this discredits our understanding of "cause" since our experience of reality reveals that concrete causes are also effects. In that case, if we wish to retain the meaning of the word "cause", then we cannot regard the supreme cause as completely different. We cannot simply nullify the normal meaning of a term and still use the same term as a basis for an analogical extrapolation to God. This would be to equivocate. If our understanding of cause necessarily involves its being understood as likewise an effect, then God as cause, albeit supreme, means that he is also an effect. Or to express this point in terms of creativity, creativity means freedom and novelty but it also signifies partial determination by previous creativities or creative acts. In being so determined, any creative act is at the same time though not in the same respect an effect. This is why Hartshorne puts much store in the claim that God is also the supreme recipient of the acts of others. "He is not merely the Origin, but also the consummatory Outcome, of the creative process; he is not simply supremely Creator, but also supreme Creature."[17] Expressed differently, activity and passivity are correlatives; what cannot act cannot be acted upon, and what cannot be acted upon cannot act. That God is cause, the creator of things does not then of necessity lead to the conclusion that he is in no sense the effect of anything.[18]

It ought to be obvious by now that Hartshorne understands God to be a creator-creature (cause-effect) and non-divine realities to be non-eminent creatures as well as non-eminent creators. God makes it possible for someone to do or not to do something. But the fact that one did something rather than something else or omitted to do it was that person's own choice. It was made by him or her and definitely *not* by God. God merely decided to make a number of alternatives open for that person.[19] Hartshorne believes in the authenticity of our freedom since we experience ourselves as in fact making decisions. If, he argues, the word "decide" has any significance at all, then we must conclude that we *do* decide, not merely that we seem to decide, and that decision-making is not God's prerogative. In fact, it is the existence of this freedom which supplies us with the foundation for grasping God's freedom or power. Doubtless, God's freedom is superior or perfect and ours is imperfect or inferior. But it is a different matter altogether to hold that we have *no* freedom at all. We do have alternatives at our disposal; otherwise, we would not be able to form any conception of God as having an infinite range of possibilities open to him.

Clearly, God's power conceived along Hartshornian lines means unsurpassable power over other genuine powers. Hartshorne is challenging the notion of a power that determines all decisions. He argues that his way of explaining God's power is consistent with God's nature. Recognizing the genuineness of the freedom of creatures does not limit God's power. God's power is indeed perfect, but the perfection of power is shown, not by taking away or preventing the freedom of others, but by fostering and inspiring that freedom. Hartshorne likens God to the creative orator, thinker and artist who inspires creative responses in others. Hartshorne's God is the supreme or perfect artist who encourages appropriate degrees of artistic originality in all creatures. "God is the unsurpassable inspiring genius of all freedom, not the self-determining coercive tyrant, or (if possible) even worse, the irresistible hypnotist who dictates specific actions while hiding his operations from the hypnotised."[20] God is also likened to rulers who are held in high esteem for their wisdom and benevolence in placing others in a position to make fruitful decisions of their own. These are the ones who awaken creativity in others. God then governs the world by inspiring us, by providing us with opportunities and by fostering creativity in us. If supreme power is understood in this way, it can only impose limits on the disagreements, conflicts or confusions among lesser powers; it cannot simply eliminate these confusions for this would require its becoming the sole power. Yet the supremacy of the

80

divine power is not being downgraded since the meaning of power is not, as is frequently held, controlling but eliciting responses which are partially self-determining or free. The ideal form of power does not monopolize power, but allots to all their due measure of creative opportunity.[21]

Hartshorne adds that not only can it be shown that there is no monopoly of power on God's part, but it can also be argued, presuming God's goodness, that he is not desirous of such a monopoly. In fact, he surpasses others in his generous willingness to delegate decision-making to others. God, we are told, inspires freedom in others thus enabling them to act freely yet in such a way that a coherent and in general harmonious world comes about. To concede all power to God is not only to misunderstand God's nature but also wrong because "unqualified monopoly is always bad, even in the eminent case".[22] There is nothing ideal about longing to possess total control and to reduce others to powerlessness. On the contrary, such a longing is symptomatic of weakness. It is the only the inferior, weak beings who yearn to be able to manipulate everything. "The Eternally Secure has no fear of letting others do some of the deciding. Eminent generosity in delegating decision-making to others and taking loving possession of the results, that is the real Eminence."[23] A concentration of decision-making in the one being is in principle undesirable because the values of life, as Hartshorne sees them, are essentially social, involving the interactions of more or less free individuals. In other words, Hartshorne gives the priority to creativity and interprets divine power in terms of the existence of this value. Power that would violate such a value is judged wrong. As he sees it, a monopoly of power is itself "the most undesirable thing imaginable; or rather it is the most unimaginable and indeed inconceivable absolutizing of an undesirable direction of thought".[24] Power cannot therefore be maximized by supposing a being who decides beforehand or eternally what happens since this would be assigning every power to that being. That would be attributing something basically immoral to him.

God's power over us is comparable to the control of one mind over another. A mind is influenced by what it knows, by its objects. Consequently, a mind which knows A but not B would be different from one which knows B but not A. A change is effected in the mind through a change in the object. Similarly by altering the object of our awareness, God influences us. God as the supreme object that is or can be given to us has only to change himself if he wants to change us. In response to God's altered state we as knowers would have to change. "God's unique power over us is his partly self-determined being as our inclusive objects of awareness."[25] God as the supreme agent therefore influences us not by controlling every detail of our action but by determining his own action which is the inclusive object of our thoughts. If we have direct awareness of the divine fiat as we have direct awareness in immediate memory of our own past experience, then this fiat will influence us. (To remember, Hartshorne explains, is to be influenced by what one remembers.) The awareness need not be conscious in the sense of being introspectively evident. We often experience the divine fiat without being cognizant of it. It is also possible to be aware of it and disobey it. But we cannot disregard it. Hartshorne maintains that to disobey is not the same as to disregard. In reacting against the command the disobedient is still influenced even though negatively. A state of rebellion or resistance to a suggestion is not the same as the state of simple unawareness of the suggestion.

Pursuing this question of God's governance of the world, Hartshorne says that God can take each successive phase of cosmic development and make unsurpassably good use of that phase in his own life and furnish the creatures with such guidance or inspiration as will optimize the ratio of opportunities and risks for the next phase. God sets the best or optimal limits to freedom. By "optimal limits" is meant that they are such that, were more freedom allowed, the risks would increase more than the opportunities, and were less freedom permitted, the opportunities would decrease more than the risks. He sets optimal limits for our free action by presenting himself as essential object. He molds us by molding himself thereby presenting at each moment a partly new ideal which influences our entire activity. "Only he who changes himself can control the changes in us by inspiring us with novel ideals for ideal occasions."[26]

God's power does not guarantee a perfection of detailed results for no power, as Hartshorne understands it, could insure the detailed actions of others. There is no complete determination of any action by one will. Rather, all realities form themselves and form each other within limits. It is the setting of these limits which constitutes the divine ordering of the world. As we have seen, causality for Hartshorne is not a rigid occurrence but an approximate and statistical pattern which allows for all sorts and levels of freedom.

Comparing his doctrine with traditional teaching, Hartshorne says that what was traditionally known as "general providence" is what he has in mind by his assertion that God decides the cosmic limits within which lie the possibilities for various happenings.[27] God accomplishes this through natural laws. Only he can decide natural or cosmic laws, which are the only laws which are always beneficent. This does not mean that all the results are good, but the advantages of having the laws outweigh the risks involved. Human laws do not compare favourably since some of the laws which human beings enact may create greater risks than opportunities. Hartshorne regards natural laws as the decisions God has already made and through which he has control over us.[28]. Man more or less fashions his human world, but he does not and could not establish the basic general order within his decisions could achieve anything. Only God could set up this general framework. But God does not institute natural laws once and for all. Natural laws, being definite ones, are not eternal but arbitrary. At due intervals God inspires the universe with new modes of behaviour which would exclude mere disorder and too exact a regularity or an eventually trivializing persistence in one type of order.[29] Hartshorne also holds that God exercises "special providence" although he does not develop this doctrine any further. He understands by it God influencing each creature to make its response to the cosmic laws.

In affirming then that God sets boundaries to the freedom of creation or that he establishes a general order, Hartshorne is refuting the view that the various forms of experience scattered through nature miraculously restrain or control themselves and each other and thus preserve a measure of harmony or mutual compatibility. They do not simply cooperate together to guarantee world order. Instead, there is a superior form of freedom, God's, which furnishes a directive which ordinary forms of freedom accept or obey. God guides all of creation and through this universal guidance lines of demarcation are established to discord and confusion. Without such guidance, order would not be possible.[30] In his benevolence God guides creation in an eloquent and appealing fashion. "God "speaks" to creatures so eloquently, beautifully, wisely, and hence relevantly to their natures that they cannot, except within narrow limits, even wish not to respond."[31] Despite divine eloquence, however, the creatures themselves are free to follow their own initiatives. God does not coerce anything, he inspires it to act in a certain way. He persuades it.

Hartshorne, however, does not deny that chance plays a certain role in creation. "Chance", he writes," is just as real as some of the atheists have been telling us during the centuries."[32] Providence is not the prevention of chance but its optimization. It checks chance occurrences. These cannot be done by chance for chance limited by chance is the same as chance not limited at all. The end result would be total chaos. Surprisingly, Hartshorne affirms the reality of chance in order to show the significance of God's providence. Through the laws of nature God puts restrictions within which the lesser agents can effectively work out the details of their existence. These limits ensure that the universal creativity does not end in universal chaos and frustration. But because of chance, there will still be elements of chaos and frustration; but they remain subordinate to the general order and harmony.

So far, it has been shown that Hartshorne's conception of the divine power envisages a real plurality of powers: there are other powers besides God. They do have an effect on God just as he has an effect on them. God exercises his power over the whole of reality, not by lording it over all like a tyrant, but by being the inclusive object of their awareness and by providing a certain framework within which creatures exercise their creativity.

Hartshorne clarifies further why his reformulation of omnipotence does not subtract anything from God's supremacy. To respond to and be influenced by the freedom or creativity of others does not lessen God's supreme position. It has frequently be held that man, not God, are responsible for human choices, at least the evil ones, and that as a result God's creative action is hindered in this way from producing a perfect world. Hartshorne fails to see how admitting change in God would limit God's supremacy any more than the aforementioned view does. Being influenced is not in itself an indication of weakness. Weakness lies in being moved in the wrong direction or disproportionately. God's unsurpassable power can be explained so as to take account of the plurality of powers as well as change in God. In this way, these so-called limitations to God's power will be seen as inherent in the meaning of omnipotence. For this reason Hartshorne sees God's power as power which is absolutely maximal or the greatest possible, but even such a power is still one power among others. Or as he puts it in another way, God is the absolute case of social influence, but even the absolute case of such an influence is still social. Hartshorne means that God recognizes the freedom of others, determining events only by putting appropriate limits to the self-determination of others.[33] To avoid the criticism that his conception of God's power demotes God, Hartshorne's strategy has been to clarify the meaning of power.[34] If power is understood in the way that Hartshorne does, then it can be seen that his version of omnipotence does not lessen God's supreme control over creation.

Earlier we noted that Hartshorne sees in human consciousness a parallel to God's power. He also draws on it to demonstrate his point that the affirmation of self-creation in creatures does not remove the uniqueness of God's power. Consciousness, he maintains, has data which it does not determine for itself, but accepts as given. Not logic, but absolutistic prejudice, has compelled philosophers and theologians to try to construe the divine as non-receptive consciousness. Hartshorne argues that the most sensitively and widely responsive individual is the very one who will be most readily and widely responded to. In responding, one appropriates the values of others, making them in some measure one's own. Thus, one could say that he who responds to all shares the values of all. This in turn would give all the best motive for responding to him inasmuch as he tends to sum up all the values around. Thus, that God is affected by the creative acts of others does not necessarily remove him from his exalted position as God. If anything, it reveals the universality and intensity of his attractiveness.

But one may well wonder whether Hartshorne considers God to be the Creator. Such a question could arise from Hartshorne's insistence on real creativity in creatures. Hartshorne reasons that apart from the notion of a first state of creation (which to him is extremely dubious and paradoxical)[35] there is no alternative to God's being in a situation of interaction with non-divine individuals. But it does not follow that God cannot be meaningfully described as the Creator. In fact, "creator" acquires a clearer meaning by analogy with human experience. God's creativity is the unsurpassable or eminent form of self-creation and creative influence over other individuals. That idea is firmly rooted in our experience of being truly creative. The task is to delineate the *distinctive* way in which God is creative. This is what Hartshorne sets out to do. Between God's form of creativity and ours there is a gap which Hartshorne does not hesitate in referring to as literally infinite. There is an unmeasurable distinction between the divine cause-effect who influences and is influenced by *every* reality and ordinary cause-effects. Ordinary cause-effects come into existence at a certain stage. They are exclusively causes of what follows them and exclusively effects of what preceded them. God, on the other hand, infinitely precedes and infinitely outlasts every other individual so that all are influenced by, and also influence, him. The uniqueness of God's creativity (which in Hartshorne's view characterizes him as the Creator) can thus be appreciated in its universality: all of reality feels his influence. This is a status not enjoyed by anyone else. We have not influenced persons who died before we were born nor can we have that much impact on those who are spatially removed from us. Again, God's uniqueness as a cause-effect can be recognized in his capacity for being affected by creatures. None of us can be directly influenced by all our contemporaries, any more than we can exert direct influence upon them all. Our limitation in the one way is the exact counterpart of our limitation in the other.[36] Hartshorne sums it up in this remark: "The preeminence of the divine influence is that (1) all things are neighbors of God, nothing is remote from him; (2) all things are appreciably and incomparably influenced by him."[37] Or as he puts it in another work, creatures are "in their humbler way creators; but God, as unsurpassably creative and influential, is *the* creator in the only sense admissible in a philosophy which makes creative freedom a universal category".[38] If then by "the Creator" is meant God's unrivaled creative activity (rather than creating from nothing) Hartshorne's interpretation does not deny that status to God. God is eminently Creator. Moreover, he claims to provide that concept with a firmer foundation since it is built on our own experience.

III. Panentheism

Hartshorne adopts the term "panentheism" to refer to his views on God and creation: in one sense God depends on the world and is therefore inclusive of it, in another sense, he is independent of it and consequently transcends it. Once again Hartshorne's distinction between God's abstract and concrete poles or aspects underlies this paradoxical statement. God as creator, insofar as this refers to his concrete aspect which changes, is indeed part of creation. However, any given creation is outside God's abstract pole.

Panentheism may be conveniently described as midway between the orthodox theistic view which maintains that God is the independent universal cause or source and the universe is his extrinsic effect or outcome (that is, the universe is "outside the divine actuality" and is not a part or constituent of it) and the pantheistic view which holds that God is the inclusive reality and that there is no ultimate cause distinct from and independent of the cosmic totality (that is, the universe and God are identical). To the question, therefore, whether God is or is not independent of the universe of entities other than himself, capable of existing without them, the orthodox theist would reply in the affirmative while the pantheist would answer negatively. Hartshorne for his part would say yes and no depending on which aspect of God's reality is at issue.

Hartshorne clarifies his position by explaining that an effect is commonly understood to imply a cause. That is, the world as effect implies a creator. But the converse relation as applied to God does not obtain for orthodox theists: God as creator or supreme cause does not need an effect. This means that while the world is qualified by its utter dependence upon God, God could have been himself, exactly as he is without any world whatever. Such a description is intended to stress the difference between an ordinary cause (with a correlative effect) and God as supreme cause (who needs no effect at all). The difference is asserted to be one in principle. In contrast, what Hartshorne is suggesting is that God's existence insofar as he is cause would make it inevitable that there be a world but only possible that there be just this sort of world. He would be independent of, and therefore would not require any particular world, but he would not be independent of world as such.[39] It will be gathered from this statement that Hartshorne means that just as the word "cause" points to an effect but not a particular effect (assuming the validity of his interpretation of causality), God *as creator* presupposes a creation but not *a particular creation*. God did not have to create this world or any given world, but he had to create some world if the term "creator" is to mean anything.

In this way God remains independent of us inasmuch as it is not essential that we exist. It is not imperative that our world exists either for God is independent of this particular world. As an independent supreme cause, "he will exist and will be himself (and would have existed and been himself) no matter what particular world exists (or had existed) or fails (or had failed) to exist".[40]. Here Hartshorne is referring to the abstract aspect of God's creative nature. In the concrete, however, God is effect as well as cause. God interacts with the world, receiving and influencing. While he is supreme power, he is one power among other, albeit lesser, powers. God thus requires other things than himself to be just what he concretely and in fact is. In this sense God indeed depends on creation.

To the doctrine then that God is creator, Hartshorne introduces a distinction which is supposed to aid us in seeing how in his way of thinking God can be independent of creation and yet be an integral part of it. He claims that it is not absurd to hold that God is truly independent of and truly dependent on creation unless by "truly" one means "in all that God is rather than in something that he is".[41] Hartshorne is utilizing the distinction between God's abstract aspect and his concrete actuality. In Hartshorne's metaphysical system then God is not and never was without a world. There is a certain necessity in creation since God could not have been without some kind of world. However, God was once without this particular world (or world state) which he now has. This world is not requisite since another world would have done. This world or any other world is contingent since everything particular or specific in the world might have been different. Or to put it in another way, from the contingency of this world one cannot conclude that God might have refrained from creating. God does not choose to have a world; he has to have one. But he has the choice of creating a particular world with such and such general characteristics.[42]

Panentheism therefore holds that God includes the world. But it sets itself apart from pantheism in that it does not maintain that God and the world are identical. Using the concept of whole-part as a model, Hartshorne explains that God is a whole whose whole-properties are distinct from the properties of the constituents. While this is true of every whole, it is more so of God as the supreme whole. Because the constituents are in the whole, what is in them is also in the whole. Thus, our misdeeds, for instance, are in God, but not *as his*. Rather, they are his misfortunes which have the effect of making his overall satisfaction less than it otherwise would be, but they do not detract from the goodness of his decisions or of his reality. For if a part decides something, the whole permits, suffers or endures the decision: it does not make the decision. The property of the part remains its own. The part is distinguishable from the whole although within it. The power of the parts is something suffered by the whole, not enacted by it.[43] The whole has properties too which are not shared by the parts. Similarly, God *as whole* possesses attributes which are not shared by his creatures.

A major feature of panentheism is its claim, already discussed, that creatures have influence on God. While creatures cannot effect the destruction of God, they determine how much each new event adds to God's concrete reality. It believes that because God can receive some benefit from our existence, there is an advantage in our existence. We decide something in God; namely, some aspect of the content of his knowledge. We perpetually create content not only in ourselves but also in God.[44] And this gives significance to our presence in this world.

Looking back at what has been discussed in this chapter, we see that Hartshorne's attempt to rethink God's power in terms of creativity credits the whole of creation with genuine freedom and power. There are varying degrees of freedom and power, but no part of reality is without these two attributes. Since the creatures' power and freedom are really their own, and not God's, there is a real plurality of powers. In the exercise of these powers, they are said to have an effect on God. This leads Hartshorne to say that God is an effect. But he is so in a truly distinctive way because only he is universally affected. He is influenced by everything that occurs with an intensity that no one else can rival. God, of course, is cause. He initiates activities and because he is supreme cause, he is always one of the agents of everything that takes place. By being the universal object of the world (Hartshorne upholds pansychism or psychicalism) he influences the whole of reality. He persuades rather than forces, he attracts rather than domineers. By means of natural laws he guides the world. This is what Hartshorne calls God's providence. In his capacity as cause, God is also unique. No matter what creatures do, they cannot challenge God's superiority for only God exercises universal influence. That God is both cause and effect is a further application of the doctrine of dipolarity. That he is universally a cause and an effect underlines the difference in principle between God and creatures.

NOTES

1. Cf. chapter 1. His most recent book, CAP, focuses on this idea.
2. It can be concluded from the above that Hartshorne maintains that all of reality is free, that nothing can be determined *wholly* by anything else.
3. "Creativity and the Deductive Logic of Causality", p. 63; Also, "Religion and Creative Experience", p. 9.
4. "Philosophy After Fifty Years", p. 143; see also LP, p. 165.
5. "Freedom is limited by acts of freedom already performed; but divine acts of cosmic relevance and influence must be included, to account for cosmic order." CSPM, p. 9. This discussion on creativity and causality is in line with what has been said regarding the nature of time in the previous chapter. The following quotation illustrates this connection: "That past events are real enables there to be a de facto totality of genuinely successive events; that "future events" are not real means that each event can constitute itself as a new synthesis, a new unified totality. "The many *become* one and are increased by one", a new inclusive unity is born; and this unity forms an item in a new many. Truth about particular events is retrospective; truth about the future is not about particular events but about tendencies, probabilities, and abstract characters bound to be embodied in some particulars or other." *Ibid.*, p. 16.
6. "Philosophy After Fifty Years", p. 143.
7. "Can Man Transcend his Animality", p. 216.
8. "Real Possibility", p. 599. This point is made by Hartshorne in various other writings.
9. LP, p. 223.
10. PSG, p. 501.
11. "Religion in Process Philosophy", pp. 255 – 256. In "Creativity and the Deductive Logic of Causality", Hartshorne tries to show that deductive logic gives credibility to his view of causality.

    From the perspective of what we know of causes and effects, he writes: "Events in their concreteness are never known in antecedent events, whereas they are habitually known in subsequent ones (more or less directly by either memory or perception)". *Ibid.* p. 67. Hartshorne means that causes are ontologically prior to effects, i.e. they are actual before the effects, but that effects are logically prior to their causes in the sense that the causes are known in the effects. He compares the relation of cause and effect to our knowledge of a past event in relation to a present one. "The past is cognitively derived from the present by abstracting from that in the past which is novel. To realize today what yesterday was like we must drop out part of what we know about today's experiences. The full strength is in the present; it was in no sense in the past." p. 67. Further on, he writes: "When we know what it is to be an effect, then we can also, by logical principles, derive what it is to be a cause, for that is the simpler case. A cause defines a set of possible effects, a set which, though it may not yet have an actual member, yet is bound to acquire one." p. 68.
12. "Beyond Enlightened Self-Interest", p. 314. Hartshorne has espoused a psychicalistic view of reality in several works.
13. "Process and the Nature of God", p. 136.
14. DR, p. 138.
15. "The New Pantheism – II", p. 143; OTM, pp. 10 – 26.
16. "Tillich and the Other Great Tradition", p. 248.
17. CSPM, p. 15.
18. MV, p. 109. According to Hartshorne, the universal literal definition of cause is a *sine qua*

non or necessary condition. It is a relation holding between concrete actualities, states or events. This definition of cause applies to God, too.

19. One can also express Hartshorne's view in the language of stimulus-response. Hartshorne holds that the precise response of the creatures cannot be determined by divine creative power just as no stimulus can absolutely determine a response. Rather, the response determines itself. But what the stimulus does is to lay down the range of possible responses. In the same way God determines what creatures can do, but only they determine what they actually do. This is true for every creature, even those in the lowest rung.

    Hartshorne is emphatic about the universality of freedom and creativity. In an article "Freedom, Individuality, and Beauty in Nature", he illustrates how this element of unpredictability can be detected in bird-song. Hartshorne is an amateur ornithologist and has published on this subject.

20. "Divine Absoluteness and Divine Relativity", p. 169. Hartshorne is critical of the theory (which he associates with Thomism) that God causes our acts but causes them as free. Freedom is taken to mean to act thus when it was really possible for the agent to have refrained from so acting. Hartshorne interprets this theory to imply that God causes us to act in a definite manner yet in such a way that we might not have acted thus. As an explanation, he finds this theory unenlightening since we are either free *or* not free, the decisions are either ours *or* not ours. But if by "causes" Agguinas meant "gives all the necessary conditions for or makes possible", then Hartshorne would agree with him. However, he thinks that Agguinas meant "gives sufficient condition for or makes actual". This second meaning contradicts freedom.

21. "Biology and the Spiritual View of the World: a Comment on Dr. Birch's Paper", p. 409: OTM, pp. 10 – 26.

22. "The Dipolar Conception of God", p. 281.

23. "Religion in Process Philosophy", p. 263.

24. "A New Look at the Problem of Evil", p. 202.

25. DR, p. 139.

26. *Ibid.*, p. 142.

27. "Religion in Process Philosophy", p. 263; also "The Dipolar Conception of God", p. 283.

28. "A New Look at the Problem of Evil", p. 206.

29. "The Divine Relativity and Absoluteness", pp. 136 – 137; cf. also "Order and Chaos", pp. 253 – 267.

30. "Religion and Creative Experience", p. 10.

31. "Religion in Process Philosophy", p. 261.

32. DR, p. 137; also "Outlines of a Philosophy of Nature, Part II", p. 385. We shall return to this topic in the next chapter when we examine Hartshorne's solution to the problem of evil.

33. DR, p. 138.

34. Bernard Meland develops this meaning of power in his "Two Conceptions of Power", *Process Studies*, vi, i (Spring, 1976), pp. 5 – 32.

35. Hartshorne finds the traditional phrase *creatio ex nihilo* to indicate God's activity as Supreme Cause to be confusing: "Here we encounter the famous phrase, *creatio ex nihilo*. God deals with no material in His decisions, he just decides: say that there is to be light, and there is light. I believe that this phrase, *ex nihilo*, supposed to emancipate theology from Greek conceptions, merely confuses the essential issues. I am a creature created by God: am I created out of nothing? If so, then I was not created by using my parents, for they were by no means nothing; Either my parents were genuinely causative of me, or they were not. If they were, then God plus nothing was not the cause; if my parents were *not* part-causes of me,

then by the same reasoning, the creatures are never causes of anything. But in that case, how do we know what we mean by cause?... If my parents were partly causative of me, then, generalizing this point, in all cases of creation (other than that of a hypothetical first state of creaturely reality) God was supreme, but not sole cause." "Man's Fragmentariness", p. 22. It must be pointed out that the phrase *creatio ex nihilo* as used by many traditional theologians refers to the first stage of creation. There are secondary causes as well, although Hartshorne insists that this phrase was given an ambiguous meaning to which Hartshorne's example of parental causality would belong. Hartshorne's criticism is more applicable to an interpretation of *creatio ex nihilo* as "absolute dependence on God", a view held by some theologicans. However, he is right in claiming that there is no basis in our experience for this notion. It may be possible to express God's creative action as differing from ours in a more experiential way rather than through the notion of *creatio ex nihilo*. This is what Hartshorne is attempting.

36. "Tillich and the Other Great Tradition", p. 259; "The God of Religion and the God of Philosophy", p. 164.

37. "Religion in Process Philosophy", p. 258.

38. "Paul Weiss's *The God We Seek*," p. 112.

39. PSG, p. 501; also "Pantheism", pp. 233 – 234.

40. PSG, p.501. If God and creation are not identical, then the question of how one conceives the entity inclusive of God *and* creation arises. Hartshorne can think of three possibilities: 1) God has the world as a constituent of his own total reality; 2) the world has God, in his total reality, as its constituent; 3) a third nameless entity has both. What follows from this classification of alternatives is that God in his total reality must either *be* a constituent or *have* constituents. If one maintains that God is a constituent, then it seems that something is greater than God. This is an alternative which would contradict God's unsurpassability. On the other hand, if one opts for the second alternative, i.e. that God has constituents, then God in his total reality is the most complex of beings. This is in effect how Hartshorne understands God. To the question as to how one can conceive the entity which includes God and creation, Hartshorne's reply is that the togetherness of Creator and creature is itself the inclusive creature and is also the inclusive reality. Hartshorne identifies this as God because in creating the world, he creates a new total reality which is himself as enriched by the world. Since the "total reality" is never simply the same twice over and since God must be the inclusive reality, then every time we refer to him we refer to a new divine totality, even though embodying the same individuality or essence. LP, p. 271.

41. PSG, p. 505; also "The Divine Relativity and Absoluteness", p. 29.

42. Hartshorne comments: "It is one thing for an agent to have freedom to do this or to do that instead; it is another for the agent to have freedom to do nothing. What is the value of the alleged freedom not to act?" AW, p. 16. This is why Hartshorne argues that even if God had decided not to create any world, this decision would itself have constituted a world-state for him.

43. PSG, p. 511; also "Deity as the Inclusive Transcendence", pp. 158 – 160.

44. "The Development of Process Philosophy", p. 52.

CHAPTER 6

GOD'S GOODNESS

In the chapter on "God's Reality" it was suggested that Hartshorne's emphasis on God's relativity or relatedness is designed to bring to the fore the religious claim that God really loves us. To regard God as absolute in all respects is to violate this basic belief in God's all-pervading love. In this chapter, we shall examine what Hartshorne says regarding divine goodness and love as well as on the problems of evil and immortality.

I. God's Love

That God is love is part of Christian teaching. Arguably it can be found in the doctrines of other religions. Hartshorne aims to substantiate this teaching in his definition of perfect or divine love as "absolute adequacy to the object".[1] He understands love as acting upon adequate awareness of others, awareness at least as adequate ideally as one has of oneself.[2] Thus, divine love is essentially social because it is "social awareness and action from social awareness".[3] God's love is affirmed to be the type of awareness that responds fully to what the other is.

This conception of divine love implies relativity or relatedness. Just as a human individual's love for another renders him or her in some genuine sense relative to the loved one so love in its eminent form makes God universally relative[4] (a point already discussed in a previous section). Hartshorne is thereby refuting the view that the highest form of love will love only an object equally exalted with itself. In experience, he asserts, one discovers that it is the highest terrestial animal that takes an interest in the welfare of the lower animals, sometimes even the lowest. Since love as Hartshorne understands it is adequate awareness of the value of others, everything — no matter how lowly it is — is completely worthy of love in the sense of having its interests fully appreciated. God's love embraces all.

This awareness of the other, which relates the lover to the loved one, also provides the reason why the other or the loved one should respond to the lover. The most sensitively and widely responsive individual is the very one who will be most readily and widely responded to. Hence, God in being uniquely good is uniquely influential. God's goodness draws creatures to him. God's worshipful excellence and beauty inspire and move creatures. Hartshorne compares God to a sensitive parent or ruler who enjoys our feelings and thoughts and responds to them. In God's case this appreciation is perfect. Because only God can appreciate us in our full worth, we unconsciously respond to this appreciation as we do not to any other.[5] The underlying argument here is that "the influential is what is in some relevant aspect good, and goodness is socially achieved, i.e. it arises through sensitivity to others".[6]

Hartshorne does not accept that admitting change in God militates against the belief in the unchanging character of God's love. One has only to turn to experience again, he says, to realize that a man's love for his friend is not defective because he must acknowledge the presence of unrealized possibilities in his friend. Nor is he any less loving because he himself changes. What Hartshorne is opposing here is the argument that God must be considered *"actus purus"* to be morally perfect. It is claimed that any attribution of change or potentiality in him would threaten the belief in God's immutable love. Hartshorne rejects this line of reasoning because in his view love has nothing to do with the possession of all possible values. In fact, the actualization of some of these possible values or unrealized capacities would provide new content for the friend's love. What Hartshorne means is that the new content of the friend's love would enrich the value of this love aesthetically but would not necessarily render it more complete or perfect in the moral sense. When Hartshorne therefore talks of change in God, he means that God acquires new content which would make him happier but not that it would make him more morally perfect. Time and again one reads in Hartshorne's works that the divine constancy posited by religion refers to his unwavering benevolence. It does not allude to the fullness of *all* values, "Clearly it is unalterableness of character, not of value, in the full sense of aesthetic enjoyment... that is meant by "in whom is no shadow of turning" ".[7]

So while it is true that God is unchangeable in that at all times he is wholly righteous and wise, it does not by any means follow that he is at all times equally and absolutely happy or that he is completely good aesthetically as well as ethically and cognitively. God's love for us which puts him in a certain relationship with us changes, aesthetically, in accordance with our actions. Our good deeds and misdeeds really affect him; hence, his state of happiness will vary. But his state of righteousness remains inflexible despite the changes of pleasure and displeasure. In fact, it is because God stays equally righteous in attitude that he must change in total value-experience in appropriate accordance with variations in the objects of his love. The wicked, stupid or indifferent person may be unmoved by deterioration or progress in other men

whereas the perfectly righteous and wise individual cannot be thus in-
sensitive. Changes which really make a difference to the value of reality must
make a difference to God.[8] In other words, Hartshorne is saying that God's
relativity (or changing aspect) does not endanger the belief in God's perfect
love so long as the distinction is held between the moral sense of this love and
its aesthetic sense.[9] Consequently, while God's perfection excludes his being
morally depraved, it does not eliminate aesthetic or physical evil from his
reality inasmuch as he is a sympathetic participant in our sufferings. The
nature of knowledge is such that concrete knowledge of suffering is in some
sense sharing in that suffering. God's knowledge is so concrete and intimate
that he is united with the sufferings of creatures much more fully than any
sympathy of ours can unite us with those suffering individuals we care about.
God does not simply know *that* we suffer, he is aware of our actual pain and
misery in their concreteness. God cannot remain aloof in the face of real
suffering.[10]

God's love has sometimes been contrasted with non-divine love in that his
love is said not to spring from need and is consequently unselfish while non-
divine love is supposed to come from need and is therefore selfish. If this were
true, then Hartshorne's God would be selfish inasmuch as he needs us to be
happier. If indeed genuine love overflows from a purely self-sufficient being
who derives nothing from anyone else, then the love of Hartshorne's God
would be suspect. Hartshorne retorts that need and self-sufficiency have
several senses and everything depends upon discriminating them. "God
"needs" only one thing from the creatures: the intrinsic beauty of their lives,
that is, their own true happiness, which is also his happiness through his
perfect appreciation of theirs."[11] Such an appreciation *is* love rather than a
motive to love. God needs us not because without us he would cease to exist,
but because the exact beauty of hiw own life varies with the amount of beauty
in lives generally. Experience shows us that love is social, that some sort of
value accrues to the self through the very fact that value accrues to another
self. What one does for others affects oneself. To raise the objection which
has just been referred to is to distort the real nature of love.

Another incentive for not accepting the argument that God is "purely"
altruistic in dealing with creatures is that this leads to the conclusion that
creatures can only love themselves. If God does not receive any value from us,
then in effect we ourselves are the object of our love. Yet the aim of creation,
religiously speaking, is to glorify God, not mankind or the world. Hartshorne
interprets this to mean that God *is* glorified. To construe it in any other way is
to assert that our actions have no impact on God but only on ourselves. But
this would amount to accepting a humanly self-regarding end as our final

goal. It would make man the ultimate. It could, of course, be argued that the ultimately achieved good is not man but the whole of creation. But even this is to leave us with the same conclusion: creation, not God, is the long-term end. It seems as if either God or something other than God is the final beneficiary of our achievements. Hartshorne would rather have God as that beneficiary. This is why for him God is really affected by what we do and why God could not have been just as glorious had there been no creation.

Hartshorne speaks of a certain necessity in divine goodness in that God's acts are always good and must always be so. God's unsurpassable goodness leaves him with no choice between what is morally right and what is evil even if he can choose between actions all of which are morally good. God's actions, therefore, have a necessary aspect in that God must always act unsurpassably well and be at all times morally upright. But it would be false to draw the conclusion that God's acts are in their entirety necessary. God's concrete acts are contingent. In whatever way God responds to the world, he could have responded otherwise, but not — and this is where the necessity lies — ethically better. There is never only one possible perfect solution to the problems the world poses for God. But whatever God decides on is from the moral point of view always the best. This is because in God's case unlike the human situation knowing and deciding are mutually inseparable. God cognitively grasps all actuality as actual and all possibility as possible in the most adequate fashion; in thus knowing reality, he seeks to actualize maximal possibilities of further value. Since he knows the end as it is, he has every motive there can be for seeking to actualize it. There can be no ethical appeal beyond the decision of someone who takes account of every actuality and possibility.[12]

God's contingent volitions are always good; being contingent, however, they are neither necessary nor eternal. For instance, contingent laws of nature, divinely instituted, obtain temporally and are accepted as good, there being no available alternatives and since any rule is preferable to chaos. Hartshorne likens God's contingent volitions to traffic regulations. It is necessary for the cosmos to have rules. God's contingent volitions are these rules. But others would have been just as good as — to take up the simile of traffic regulations — driving on the left, if universally accepted, would have been just as good as driving on the right. While goodness is a common property of any possible divine volitions, as of any possible acts of an ideally good and wise ruler, he is not bound to one possible course of action. Despite God's inability to choose between the greater and lesser good, he can adopt alternative ways of willing the greatest good.

On this point one question that has troubled theists is whether God could not have created us, like himself, free but necessarily virtuous beings. It has been held that although God is not free to choose between deciding rightly and deciding wrongly, he cannot be said to have less freedom. We have seen that Hartshorne concurs with this view as he says, "Being necessitated to these modes of action would still leave one with innumerable free decisions to make. God would be more, not less, free since his range of creative capacities is unsurpassable."[13] So why can we not be like God in this respect? If God can be necessarily wise and good yet free to choose among ways of being good, why not we also? Hartshorne's own answer is that it is not merely for the sake of ethical freedom that creatures are free. The basic significance of freedom is aesthetic. Concrete values are aesthetic, not ethical. There can be no necessity here. Only the abstract can be necessitated. Thus virtue can be necessary in God only because of its abstract character. Only God has that abstract character which is absolute. But the particular beauty of the cosmos is contingent even for God, and in continual process of accretion. This is why the value of God's actual experience as distinguished from his necessary virtue is likewise endlessly enriched. Furthermore, infallible goodness, like infallible wisdom and unsurpassable power are all divine attributes and belong together, indeed are one thing variously expressed. Goodness is for us – Hartshorne agrees with Niebuhr – an "impossible possibility", an ideal we try to live up to, but not being God, we may not manage to attain it. It is not automatic or guaranteed. God seeks the creatures' good as also good for God, but God has absolute appreciation of that good. This is divine appreciation. It *could not* be ours.

God's love or goodness is unique for only God is absolutely adequate to the object. In its literalness, love is God's sole privilege. There is no way anybody can outdo the absolute lovingness of God which is his holiness. Others merely approximate the ideal of seriously caring for themselves and others whereas God provides that ideal. He takes us infinitely more seriously than we do ourselves. In addition, while our love is restricted to a few, God's love is universal. He loves all the persons there ever have been or are, and will love all who will exist. God alone knows our interests, fully and concretely, and in knowing them, shares them. As has been pointed out, in him knowing and valuing are the same since there can be no duality of understanding and motivation in a being in whom both qualities are perfect. "To fully sympathize with and to fully know the feelings of others are the same relationship separable in our human case only because there the "fully" never applies."[14] We know the feelings of others but in reality only have knowledge *about* them. Our knowledge is no more than a rough estimate of how they feel. But if we knew the individuality and vividness of the feeling, the way God does, we would have that feeling, too.

God's goodness also stands out on its own in that God is always good, unlike us. Since we are fallible beings, our awareness of the object is not absolutely adequate; we require ethical rules as substitutes by which we guard against the more dangerous effects of our ignorance. We do not see the concrete situation, except with enormous and more or less wilfully selected blind spots. Rules adopted in moments of calm and disinterested reflection, serve the purpose of protecting ourselves and others against the bias of our perception and inferences. We go astray because our knowledge of reality is not necessarily the actual, concrete awareness of things, but the virtual or abstract awareness of them. Our inadequate knowledge leads to inadequate response. But where knowledge can never be inadequate, as in God's case, the response will always be adequate to the reality. Hence, he alone chooses the greatest good.[15] Only God is suitably described as goodness itself.

II. The Problem of Evil

Hartshorne's claim that God is good and necessarily so provides the justification for believing in God's indubitable love for us. Yet the fact of evil, which is present everywhere, challenges such a belief. A wholly righteous and loving God, presuming that he is also supremely powerful, would not want suffering, pain or natural disasters to happen. So why is there evil? Hartshorne is disinclined to make God the scapegoat. He insists that evil occurs because of the creativity of others. This creativity which is the condition of any opportunity for good is also responsible for the evils in the world. Briefly, there is evil because there is universal creativity.

Hartshorne thus tackles the problem of evil by reminding us that God's governance of the world cannot be conceived of as totally determining any part of it. The making of the world is not a simple act of God, but a fusion of divine and lesser acts, all in their fashion self-determining, creative or free. The world is not divinely decreed as to its details but is the result of the divine decisions plus innumerable creaturely decisions. No one agent can decide a situation since every other agent involved contributes to the decision. If all creatures are free, then no divine directive, argues Hartshorne, could do more than set boundaries to the possibilities of discord and disorder in the world. Absolute order could in no way be guaranteed, not because God is weak, but because it would not be strength to abolish creaturely freedom.[16]

Evil comes about because the partial self-determination of each and every actuality means genuine chance at the points of intersection between diverse free acts. What Hartshorne means is this: I decide my act, you decide yours, but how my act and yours flow together to constitute a new total situation neither you nor I – nor anyone, including God – decide. In short, it simply happens. Situations are never in their entirety decided by anyone. The chance coming together of various free acts is the cause of all our woes, aided here and there, no doubt, by wickedness and carelessness, but never attributable to these alone. God, in his goodness, ideally intends and ideally operates to produce the good of the creatures for themselves and for one another. So far as the divine contribution to the situation is concerned, there can be neither wickedness nor carelessness. It is not God, therefore, who is responsible for evil. Hartshorne blames chance.[17] Evils spring from chance, not from providence. This is the consequence of universal creativity. As was explained before, for Hartshorne every individual – from the atom upwards – has an aspect of self-determination or spontaneity. The intersection of two creative acts, not to mention myriads of them, is precisely due to chance. Thus, in Hartshorne's view, it is meaningless to ask why God does not control the world so that evils could not happen. Such a question would arise only if God is understood to have a monopoly of decision-making.[18] Nor can any amount of evil prove that God has willed evil since it is the chance coming together of creaturely acts which actually produce it.

Since all creatures in Hartshorne's metaphysics have some freedom, all evil can and should be viewed as deriving from unfortunate (not necessarily or in general wicked) cases of creaturely freedom. If what x decides harmonizes with what y decides, it is good luck; if it does not, it is bad luck. It really is luck for neither x nor y nor yet z (even if z is God) can simply determine that harmony shall reign. All can aim at harmony, but none can secure it, not even God, simply because the situation is such that each must decide in some measure for himself and no decision can be foreseen in their full concreteness. They cannot be foreseen, much less eternally seen, by God for until they take place they do not exist as wholly definite entities or facts. Hence, each agent must take a certain chance of discord, whatever he himself decides and however benevolent he or anyone is.[19] In spite of God's guidance therefore, some conflict and misfortunes do arise.

The world as Hartshorne views it, consists of active individuals. To be such an individual is to exercise a measure of independence that is definitely its own. The tragedy of the world is the price of this individuality. The greater the depth of individuality, the greater the possibilities for evil. It is not simply a question of moral evil (as has been understood in tradition) for even the most innocent uses of freedom involve some risk of conflict and suffering. On the other hand, the good that is in the world is also rooted in this individuality. The possibility for good is proportionate to the depth of individuality.

Without freedom with its perils there would be neither evil nor good. Creaturely freedom which gives rise to evils is an essential aspect of all good acts so that the price of a guaranteed absence of evil would be equally an absence of good. Risk of evil and opportunity for good are two facets of the one thing − multiple freedom. The justification of risk is the opportunity for good of which the risk is an inseparable aspect. The less freedom there is, the fewer the risks with a corresponding lessening in the number of opportunities for good. This is why to trivialize risks by reducing freedom is, in the last analysis, to trivialize opportunities for good.[20] God's love for creation would not allow him to deprive even the least creature of its due amount and kind of freedom. "Love cannot be less than the wish to have others exist as genuine actualities, and this means as partly selfdeciding agents, whose fortunes depend therefore in part upon themselves and their neighbors."[21]

What is required for cosmic order is not that all risk of conflict and consequent suffering be removed for that would be to exclude all reality, but that the risks be justified by the opportunities for good or significant harmonies. Hartshorne regards the laws of nature as fulfilling this function of providing a basic framework of order. Without them, there would be more possibilities for evil. But even with such a framework of order, Hartshorne concedes that the world can be realistically described as tragic. Hartshorne upholds what Einstein has denied: belief in a dice-throwing God, who takes chances on what his creatures will do under certain natural laws divinely decreed for the world. Hence, there will always be evil. Even if God had set up alternative laws (in place of the natural laws currently in operation) or certain other limitations upon creaturely freedom, there would still be risks. Any possible divine directive would still leave universal freedom and therefore universal risk. With other divine actions the risks of evil would indeed have been different. But it does not follow, and we could not possibly know, that the risks of evil, as balanced against the opportunities for good, would have been less. The underlying argument, it would appear, is that creativity would be embodied in any world that God would create. Thus, there will always be risks as well as opportunities.

To Hartshorne then the problem − or pseudo-problem as he has called it in his writings − arises because of a misconception of God's power. Evil exists not because God is too weak to prevent evil or too indifferent to try to prevent it. Rather, God's power and love are directed towards individuals who have their own independence. Otherwise, God's power would be power over nothing and his love over nothing. What is actually required is a better understanding of the meaning of power, whether divine or non-divine. Hartshorne is convinced that his interpretation of divine power as unsurpassable creativity does not attribute any weakness or indifference to God. At the same time, to credit God with perfection of power and goodness, which Hartshorne does, need not imply that the evils in the world must be his doing. For this reason Hartshorne does not accept what he thinks is a forced option between denying divine power or goodness and denying the reality of evil.

Nor can Hartshorne see how the experience of evil can imply the non-existence of God. It can legitimately do this only on the assumption that the entire absence of evil is deducible from the presence of God. But it would lead to wanting God to create individuals not only imperfect in freedom but wholly deprived of freedom, unable to make any decision except those duplicating what God decides for them. The atheistic arguments therefore assumes, in Hartshorne's opinion without grounds, that God's eminent or worshipful form of power means the kind of power which determines everything whereas it can be shown, he holds, that divine power could not possibly deprive a single creature of even the minimum of freedom. Monopolistic power able to guarantee universal harmony is a misconception of God's power and substantiates the atheistic case. For if everything is divinely arranged, why is there evil not only in human life but in all life?[22]

Evils are unfortunate consequences of creativity and hence, are to be expected. This situation is somewhat analogous to an artist's picture which cannot contain all colors nor all shapes. To preserve its beauty, it has to be rather severely limited. The contrasting shades draw out and intensify certain aspects and thus maintain aesthetic balance. Yet it would be a mistake to conclude from this analogy that beauty necessitates some contrast between good and evil in the world. Hartshorne is more inclined to argue that nobody, even God, has to deliberately produce evil for this purpose. It is the inevitable outcome of freedom rather than a conscious decision on God's part. It is an indirect effect rather than an objective. It is goodness, beauty and harmony that have to be sought after even if evil will still result.[23]

The theory that evil is good in disguise is rejected by Hartshorne because ultimately it reduces human choice to absurdity. It would be tantamount to asserting that no matter what we do, the result would be exactly the same. There would be no distinction between what is good and what is evil, between the good that one has chosen and the evil that one may have opted for. If evil were good in disguise, then our actions which are said to be evil would be in accordance with the divine plan. Otherwise, they would not have happened. On this view serving God is equivalent to doing what one happens to be doing. Since one's actions will always be the fulfilment of God's wishes, there can be nothing wrong with them. To put this in another way, if evil is alleged to be disguised good, then it would have to be considered as part of the divine plan. But this being the case, no matter what we do, be it good or apparently evil, we cannot claim credit for it. There would be no such thing as human choice for we have merely fulfilled the divine decree. What is even more problematic with this view, in Hartshorne's opinion, is the difficulty of distinguishing between such a God and the sadist who finds evil to his liking. For after all, it seems that God deliberately designs evil if it is seen to be an integral part of his world-plan.[24]

Hartshorne is also critical of the view that evils are punishments from God. This explanation of particular evils in terms of individual deserts meted out by God is a misuse of the idea of providence. God for Hartshorne is neither a wise sadist nor a detached magistrate, torturing us for some good end. "Cosmic governance is not a magnified law court."[25] Hartshorne also takes exception to the view that evil is permitted rather than intended by God. This suggests that God has the option of constantly depriving creatures of their own decision-making whereas God could not make our decisions for us. If such were possible, the decisions we make would not really be ours. Worse than that, God would not have creatures if he took away their freedom. As Hartshorne sees it, not only does God not desire evil, he does not allow it, either. What he wants is that there be opportunities for good and that these, as much as is possible, in each case, should be fulfilled. Given freedom, there will certainly be some evils. But so far as one is ethical — and God is definitely so — then it is the good that one seeks.[26] God does not permit evil as if there were some justification for it.

By universalizing creativity and by re-interpreting God's power instead Hartshorne hopes to demonstrate how evil can still be given a plausible explanation in a theistic context. Furthermore, he is cognizant of the inner conflicts in man which sometimes end up in evil deeds. As he has shown man's exercise of freedom is often made in comparative ignorance of the interests of others, unlike God who is fully aware of the values of others and always desirous of what is best for them. The world is tragic, not only because conflict is inevitable between free and ignorant beings, but also because there is an inner conflict in man between their will to serve a common good and their desire to promote a private or tribal goal. Some conflicts and pain often arise because a less destructive or more fruitful alternative was not chosen. Here there is a deliberate choosing of the greater evil and the lesser good. Apart from God, every free agent is fallible both in understanding and in ethical goodness. Hence, neither destructive folly nor damaging wickedness can be entirely excluded. In short, the existence of evil can also, in many cases, be traced back to man's perversity.

That there are lesser but genuine forms of creativity accounts for the existence of evil. But the existence of supreme creativity, namely God, explains how there can be much goodness in the world.[27] With God there is order in the world so that, notwithstanding the evils, good is a definite possibility. The chances of evil are subordinate to the chances for good. Hartshorne confidently proclaims that nature is full of goodness, harmony and joy.[28] Thus, while accepting the reality of evil, he nonetheless regards God's existence as providing solid grounds for optimism.

There is further incentive for such optimism when we reflect on the nature of this God. As all-knowing, God knows our suffering and is thereby internally affected by it. This is why it can truly be believed that God participates in our suffering. Not only does he contain our suffering, he also suffers. It is in accord with his nature to sympathize in this way. But evil in the sense of wickedness is not in God's character at all although such evil is included in God's reality but not in a way that he can be depicted as evil.

To sum up Hartshorne's thinking on the problem of evil, one could turn to his own words:

...My view of the problem of evil is: (a) it is a pseudo-problem due to a pseudoconcept of omnipotence or divine power; evil springs from creaturely freedom, and without such freedom there could be no world at all; (b) creaturely freedom capable of producing evil, at least in the form of suffering is universal to the creation, not confined to man or rational animals, or even to animals; (c) God's supremacy consists, not in his making the creatures' decisions for them, but in his setting abstract limits of law to creaturely decisions, and in his ideally free evaluation of the results so that they acquire permanent meaning; finally, (d) God shares in all suffering since he cherishes all creatures, so that he may be seen as the ideal companion in sorrow as well as joy. God would be masochistic as well as sadistic, if it were true that he deliberately caused us to suffer. But he is neither, for no concrete evil is divinely decided, whether as punishment, means of spiritual education, or in view of any other end. God sees no other way to have creatures or any world. The risks of freedom are inseparable from freedom, and the price of its opportunities.[29]

III. Immortality

In many a religious thought the belief in God's goodness which seems threatened by the presence of evil in the world finds support in the doctrine of a final justification after death. It is believed that the good will ultimately be rewarded while the evil ones will be punished. Although evil deeds are seen as reaping rewards in this life, it is held that this will be rectified in the next world. Full justice will be meted out and the scales of justice will tipped over in favor of the good and the deserving.

But Hartshorne takes issue, as mentioned earlier, with this interpretation of God's goodness and justice. He points out, that the chance of doing that which is right and of loving God and others is here and now. At the same time rewards and punishments can be expected in this life. If on earth one cannot find value in being good or disvalue in being or doing ill, then Hartshorne doubts whether one will come across it in any heaven or hell. Having said that, Hartshorne wishes to stress that love should be the motivating force of what we do, not the scheming for reward or avoidance of eternal punishment. He writes, "If love is not its own reward, then God is not love."[30] Instead, God would simply be the dispenser of awards and demerits. Yet Hartshorne's rejection of post-mortem rewards or punishments is not a denial of the possible good or bad consequences of our actions which will outlast us. All he wishes to emphasize is that our reward is *now* while we are performing the actions. We may direct our attention to a future reward, e.g. a benefit to someone who survives us, but this present aiming at something in the future is the source of our joy. In one respect, the future good accruing to someone else will be our reward; but it is one which we can enjoy only in anticipation as we could be gone before it happens. Our participation is now rather than later. Thus, Hartshorne cannot accept the argument that since many do not have a fair lot in this life, justice demands that they should have another and better opportunity elsewhere. He adds that in any sphere there will be chance, hence good and bad luck due to creativity. The demand for justice, i.e. to each according to his deserts, is not an ultimate axiom valid cosmically or metaphysically.

Hartshorne's neoclassical metaphysics lends no support to the doctrine of personal immortality on which the belief in post-mortem rewards and punishments stands. He is conscious that his view means a serious conflict with religious sentiment although he is unsure whether the conflict is all that serious now.[31] He has some harsh words for this doctrine, especially when taken in conjunction with the notion of divine justice expressed as the apportioning of rewards and punishments after death for human actions. He sees in it "substantial elements of irrationality, not in the sense of doctrines above reason but of doctrines below and contrary to it".[32] In an approving tone he quotes Berdyaev who refers to it as "the most disgusting morality ever conceived".[33] Hartshorne looks on personal immortality as a rival to belief in God rather than a logical consequence of it since it seems to enshrine self-interest as ultimate.[34] The believer is led to expect an everlasting award in comparison with which nothing on earth would or could be as significant. Hartshorne also finds fault with this doctrine because one cannot talk of an identical self reaping rewards or punishments. "Each momentary agent and sufferer", he says, "is numerically new, from which it follows that the I which now acts never can receive either reward or punishment, beyond the intrinsic reward or punishment of acting and experiencing as it now does. The account is immediately closed. Anything one demands for the future is demanded for another, even though this other is termed "one's self"".[35] In Hartshorne's view, the whole theory of heaven and hell seems largely to be the result of the concept of personal "substance" which he questions. Evidently, Hartshorne's counterargument depends on the acceptability of his own interpretation of personal identity discussed previously.

One answer that has been put forward to this question is social immortality: ultimate value is preserved by posterity. But Hartshorne does not agree that this answers the quest for ultimacy. It may be true that our acts will resonate in future human beings. For example, readers of books which we may have written, the spectators of the buildings which we may have erected, our children who will benefit from our efforts – these will furnish the actual or at least potential realization of our future reality as individuals who have existed. But Hartshorne is dissatisfied with this answer because no one can know us fully while we live and less so after our deaths. Many details about our lives are missed even by the closest of our contemporaries and not surprisingly by posterity. Generations are frequently almost wholly unconscious or unappreciative of the deeds of previous generations. The simple fact is that we, individually and collectively, forget. Our experiences seem to perish almost as fast as they occur because we fail to remember much about them. At any moment everything except a tiny portion of our past life is erased from our memories. Future generations will hardly be better in this respect. Hartshorne asks, what will most of our lives mean to those who come after us, who will know little of these lives and care less?[39] Besides, there does not seem to be much evidence that mankind will continue forever. It is doubtful whether the human species is literally immortal even if species do last longer than individuals. Over every generation hangs the apparently inevitable doom that sometime there will be the last generation. When that happens, then the question of the ultimate value of our lives and deeds resurfaces. Thus, granting that our lives may leave their mark long after we ourselves are gone, we nonetheless cannot suppose that humanity would be capable of preserving for all time this monument of ours. To suppose so is to blur the known traits of humanity.[39]

Hartshorne sees the question of ultimacy or immortality as pressing us towards the theistic solution. After all, it is God, not man, who never dies. Death is a reminder that beings who are limited in time cannot be the final end. Deathless existence is God's prerogative. Moreover, God is the only knower whose knowledge is fully adequate to the happenings in the world, able fully to grasp and evaluate their qualities, richness and beauty.[40] For this reason, Hartshorne argues that values are permanent not as human but divine possessions.[41] Only God can be the final recipient of our achievements, the ultimate beneficiary by which their value is measured. Our achievements have eternal significance only if there is an inclusive consciousness, such as God's, which enjoys and appreciates their having occurred. God's continued existence and unsurpassable memory mean that he will cherish us no matter how long we have been dead. In acquiring us as we are on earth he acquires us forevermore. As Hartshorne himself expresses it: "If we will have value in the memories of friends and admirers who survive us, much more can we have value in the consciousness of God, who endures forever, and who alone can fully appreciate all that we have been, felt or thought".[42] Hartshorne can therefore say that very literally we exist to enhance, not simply to admire or enjoy, the divine glory. Ultimately, we are contributors to the ever-growing divine treasury of values. We serve God; our final and inclusive end is to contribute to the divine life. Because of this, there is something perpetual in each entity in that it will be preserved in God.[43]

To appreciate this theistic yet non-conventional version of ultimacy, it should be recalled that for Hartshorne reality contributes to God's actuality. God in his concreteness is really related to us. Since the claim is made by Hartshorne that God in his relative aspect loves and genuinely becomes or acquires novel values, he has relevance to human aspirations that a merely absolute and changeless deity cannot have. A God who cherishes us and is not once for all complete, but is ever enriched with new values can and would acquire value from his awareness of our experiences as they occur. There is no futility in our existence, Hartshorne consoles us, if indeed all the human living as actually lived has passed into the imperishable reservoir of enjoyed experiences which is God's actuality. Hartshorne's dipolar God is the cherisher of all achieved actualities. Hence, all of one's life can be a "reasonable, holy and living sacrifice to God". The value of this sacrifice hinges on the sort of life we have lived. A poor, thin or discordant life, made so by lack of generous openness to others or to the beauty of the world and the divine harmony pervading all seemingly insignificant things, is a poor gift to the divine valuer of all things. What we do with our lives will decide what God will remember of us. Hartshorne is quite graphic in his description: "One might say that we mold the picture that will forever hang in the divine mansion. God will make as much out of the picture in beholding it as can be made, but how much can be made depends upon the picture and not merely upon the divine insight in seeing relations and meanings."[44] It may not be our privilege to live everlastingly – that is God's – but at least we can ensure our lives to have been well-lived within God's own life. In Hartshorne's philosophy the final significance of all we do is in the contribution our lives can make to God, the Eminent Life, in whom all experience once it has occurred, is perpetuated. Thus, it matters a great deal whether we have done well or not, whether we have led happy lives or not. In the final analysis, it matters to God. Hartshorne adds that if we love God, then it matters to us now; we would care about what we do because of the impact that we have on God.[45]

According to Hartshorne then, our immortality is God's memory of us. Because he knows us adequately he can appreciate totally the worth of each moment of our lives. The passing moment is captured forever by him who knows how to do justice to all its beauty and value. Because our memories are faint and selective we can never be in that position. Yet our forgotten experiences are not lost since they are additions to the experiences of God, the cosmically social and all-cherishing being, to whom all hearts – not only as they are but as they have been – are open. The essential meaning of our immortality is the everlasting transparency of our lives to the divine.[46]

A possible objection to this interpretation of our immortality is that it seems to immortalize God's memory of us rather than us. Hartshorne replies that this objection bares a secret egotism since it shows that what we have really wanted is to be the Immortal Person ourselves, or that we have regarded God, not as the end of ends, but as means to our own end, namely, the achievement of permanence. We wish, it would appear, to set ourselves up as immortal gods, rivaling God. As Hartshorne points out, "If we claim immortality for ourselves, then God is needed only as support for our self-fulfillment."[47] Hartshorne finds this blasphemous.

Because life is contributory, ultimately to God, Hartshorne admits that there is some truth in the doctrine of social immortality despite his reservations about it. It would be one-sided, he says, to contrast social immortality (the non-religious form of everlasting life) with theistic immortality (the kind he is espousing) for the two need not be regarded as incompatible. Social immortality can be redefined in theistic terms. God whose future is endless and who alone fully appropriates and adequately appreciates our ephemeral good is the social being who is neighbor to all of us. Social immortality, as Hartshorne sees it, is literal immortality in God as *the* neighbor. For he alone is exempt from death and able to love all equally. "He is the definitive "posterity"."[48] Our abiding value is indeed what we give to posterity, to the life that survives us; but the permanence of life's values cannot consist simply in what each of us does for our human posterity. In the long run, this is God.

Hartshorne's interpretation of immortality is complemented by his doctrine of the immortality of the past which asserts that what once existed but now seems to have ceased to exist is not reduced to nothingness. Strictly speaking, something cannot become nothing. Death is not the total annihilation of an individual. An individual becomes, he does not "decome" or "unbecome"; he is created, he is not destroyed or "de-created". This doctrine of the immortality of the past leads on to the doctrine of God's memory of us since to conceive the full possession of the past one needs to envisage a perfect form of memory, one without any admixture of forgetfulness. This is divine memory.[49] Since human memory is incomplete, the true basis of permanence is complete memory. Only an ideally perfect memory could constitute the adequate conservation of experience in full vividness and value. We can, in the profoundest sense, "live forever" if and only if we are cherished by an imperishable and wholly clear and distinct retrospective awareness which we may call the memory of God.[50]

What Hartshorne has to say on immortality, therefore, implies that death is not the final end although it is the "fixing of the concluding page to one's book of life".[51] That there is death is not an indication that God does not love us despite the persistent feeling among many people that if God loves us he will not suffer us to be destroyed. But as far as Hartshorne is concerned, this cannot be true because death does not represent destruction but only the setting of a definitive limit. It is not the obliteration of what has existed. Thus for him death does not militate against the belief in God's goodness.

A useful summary of the above discussion is provided by Hartshorne himself:

I mentioned a non-conventional view of personal immortality. This is the Bergsonian-Whiteheadian doctrine of the cumulative nature of becoming, of "The immortality of the past". It is our earthly lives that are imperishable, our actual experiences. They persist as background, content, memories, perceptions, through all future experience. True, these memories and perceptions are mostly, in ordinary cases, very faint. But according to theistic philosophy there is also the extraordinary or "eminent" case, divine perception and memory. Thanks to it, the full vividness of our experiences can "live forevermore". Is this personal immortality? If one's actual concrete experiences are not personal, I do not know what would be. They represent all that one actually is. Beyond our actual experiences our personalities are simply potentialities for experience. Those who want to "wake up" in heaven are not asking for the preservation of their earthly actuality; rather they ask for the actualization of additional possibilities. I hold with Whitehead that actual occurrences, experiences, are the concrete entities and that all actual value is in these. If immortality is preservation of the already created, Whitehead's view furnishes it. If it is opportunity for further creation of ourselves by ourselves, the view does not furnish it. But we should know what we are asking, whether preservation or additional creation... The future of religion will depend in no small part upon whether people can realize that preservation of what we create in ourselves and others suffices to give life a lasting meaning, and that to ask also for endless further self-creation is not easily distinguishable from asking that we should be God, who indeed is endlessly self-creative.[52]

We have arrived at the end of our investigation of Hartshorne's attempt to provide a philosophical framework for the religious idea of God. What emerges is the concept of a dipolar God. Hartshorne's contention is that this alternative conception of God is closer to what religion understands by "God" compared to the classical notion of the absolute, immutable God.

NOTES

1. MV, p. 165.
2. *Ibid*.
3. *Ibid*., p. 173.
4. "Whitehead in French Perspective", p. 580.
5. "Religion and Creative Experience", p. 10. cf. *Infra*., p. 80.
6. "Religion and Process Philosophy", p. 261.
7. MV, p. 158.
8. *Ibid*., p. 110; cf. also "Reflections on the Strength and Weakness of Thomism", p. 54.
9. In many of his writings Hartshorne seems to equate God's righteousness with God's love. But in MV, p. 130, he states that "love" implies the final concrete truth. By this he means that God *is* love and not just loving, as he is merely righteous or wise (though in the supreme or definitive way). Hartshorne's reason for this qualification is that in love the ethico-cognitive and aesthetic aspects of value are both expressed.
10. "A New Look at the Problem of Evil", p. 207.
11. MV, p. 163.
12. DR, pp. 124 – 125. Hartshorne's doctrine of dipolarity means that there is a necessary aspect and a contingent aspect of God's goodness and love.
13. "Divine Absoluteness and Divine Relativity", p. 166.
14. MV, p. 162.
15. DR, p. 126. It appears to me that what Hartshorne means by the "greatest good" is what God *actually* chooses. Only in this way is it reconcilable with God's freedom to choose among alternative ways. If what God *could have* chosen can still be described as "the greatest good", then God, given his unsurpassable knowledge, would have chosen it. Thus, I interpret Hartshorne as saying that the standard of goodness is closely identified with God's actual choice.
16. "Religion and Creative Experience", p. 11.
17. Cf. "Religion in Process Philosophy", p. 263. Hartshorne elaborates on his solution to the problem of evil in a number of writings.
18. "The Nature of Philosophy", p. 13.

19. "A New Look at the Problem of Evil", pp. 205 – 206.
20. "Two Forms of Idolatry", p. 14.
21. "Love and Dual Transcendence", p. 96.
22. CSPM, p. 6.
23. "Answers to Questions", p. 48. (See, "God and the Social Structure of Reality")
24. "The Modern World and a Modern View of God", p. 77.
25. NTOT, p. 121.
26. "The Dipolar Conception of God", p. 286. Hartshorne writes that perhaps there is no answer to *why* God sends us evils since God does not send them at all. Rather, he establishes an order in which creatures can send each other particular good and evils. NTOT, p. 120.
27. "Philosophy After Fifty Years", p. 145; also, "A New Look at the Problem of Evil", p. 211.
28. *Ibid.*, pp. 206 – 211.
29. LP, p. 254.
30. *Ibid.*
31. According to Hartshorne, "neither Tillich nor Niebuhr is clearly committed to the conventional ideal of immortality. Do most church members really live to get themselves (or others) into heaven or avoid getting into hell?" "Philosophy After Fifty Years", p. 147.
32. "A Philosopher's Assessment of Christianity", p. 175.
33. "Religion and Creative Experience", p. 11. Yet in other writings he appears to be more open to the question of personal immortality; see, for instance, LP, p. 253.
35. "Religion in Process Philosophy", p. 264. This point should be taken in conjunction with Hartshorne's interpretation of "personal identity". Cf. *Supra*, pp. 44 – 45.
36. "The Significance of Man in the Life of God", pp. 40 – 41.
37. MV, p. 156. Hartshorne continues, "Those who object that in the meantime these values will have been really enjoyed seem to me unconsciously to smuggle in an assumption contrary to the hypothesis. For if, after the hypothetical catastrophe it would indeed be true that values would "have been" realized, and this would be better than if they "had not been" realized, then surely some value would have escaped the allegedly complete catastrophe, namely, a sort of anonymous reminiscent savoring of past enjoyments." *Ibid.*
38. RSP, p. 49.
39. NTOT, p. 57.
40. "Beyond Enlightened Self-Interest", p. 311; "A Metaphysics of Individualism", p. 145.
41. "Process Philosophy as a Resource for Christian Thought", p. 48.
42. "The God of Religion and the God of Philosophy", p. 156. Hartshorne sums up his stance in the following quotation: "…In abstraction from God, and in view of the mortality of all others than God, in view also of the uncertainties of life, what definite idea can there be of future good as enhanceable by our choices? We help our children; but they will eventually turn into dust, as the Bible has it. And who can tell what may happen to the human species, with or without our help? Besides, all actual good is enjoyed good… and who can enjoy the "good of all" in all the future? Without God there is no definite universal good to which all may contribute. Each of us possesses only his own good; less than that, only his own good at the given moment. Where and whose is the good of all throughout their careers? It is in God that the many goods are united and made permanent. Only in God and his appreciation does it all "add up" to anything." "Paul Weiss' *The God We Seek*", p. 110.
43. Hartshorne maintains that we can at least *believe* that God will remember us forever in an unsurpassable fashion. To deny that this can or should be important to us is to make into a riddle the fact that we often go to great lengths to try to insure that human beings will, in a far from unsurpassable or everlasting fashion, remember our lives and actions. "The Dipolar Conception of God", p. 288.

44. LP, p. 257.

45. "Some Thoughts on "Souls" and Neighborly Love", p. 147; "Man's Fragmentariness", p. 23.

46. "Religion in Process Philosophy", p. 265. Such an understanding of immortality is dependent on a particular idea of God. Hartshorne expresses this point succinctly, "Only a socially-sensitive, all-retaining memory can give life a long-run meaning, and only a socially constituted deity can have such a memory." RSP, p. 50.

47. "Man's Fragmentariness", p. 23.

48. "Beyond Enlightened Self-Interest", p. 309.

49. Cf. "El valor como disfrute del contraste y la teoría acumulativa del proceso", p. 193; "The Development of Process Philosophy", p. 59.

50. "The Buddhist-Whiteheadian View of the Self and the Religious Traditions", p. 301. The demand that the past should survive is not merely an emotional one, but also a logical one, as was explained earlier. After events have happened, it should always be true that they have happened. "Truth must be true of reality. If the reality keeps fading out, so must truth. But what then would make it true that it had faded? Thus the literal immortality of the past, in principle accounted for by memory and perception, but adequately only in and adequate memory or perception, is required to explain what "truth" means." Ibid. Cf. also "The Structure of Metaphysics...", pp. 233 – 234; OTM, p. 34.

51. LP, p. 253. Hartshorne feels that it is more certain that there can be no subtraction. That there can be no addition, however, he is less sure, saying that personal survival after death with memory of personal life before death is "hardly an absurdity". He finds that the analogy to a butterfly with its succession of bodies, while remote and implausible, is not necessarily strictly inapplicable. What looks to him like a genuine impossibility is the view that there will never be any end, that the chapters of our book will be infinite in number. My reading of Hartshorne on this point is that he is really indefinite about the validity of personal immortality. He is inclined to deny it, as has been noted a few pages back, because he wants to argue that man's fragmentariness means temporal as well as spatial limitedness.

52. "Philosophy After Fifty Years", pp. 148 – 149.

CONCLUDING REMARKS

In the introduction to this study, it was stated that recent discussions in the philosophy of religion and theology have been to some extent centered on the concept of God. It can no longer be taken for granted that "God" is a consistent and clear idea. The inevitable consequence has been that a number of thinkers have proposed various ways of understanding the term God.

One such attempt is Hartshorne's neoclassical or process concept of God which has been the subject of this book. Hartshorne, we recall, aims to provide us with a different *way* of articulating what religion means by "God". He wants to bridge the gap between the God of religion and the God of philosophers. His work has elicited both positive and negative responses.[1]

By way of conclusion, two comments are worth making here. First, the acceptability of Hartshorne's concept of God depends largely on the validity of the argument that one can make a distinction between one's basic concrete experience and the articulation, particularly in an intellectual sense, of that experience. It will be recalled that this distinction plays a crucial role in Hartshorne's approach to the problem.[2] If such a distinction is possible, then we must bear in mind that a philosophical expression is not to be confused with one's basic experience. Some philosophical conceptualities will be found to be much more suitable than others in conveying what one intuitively holds. But the expression is not the intuition itself. It would be regrettable if one replaced the other. The process idea of God should therefore be accepted or rejected for what it is: a philosophical expression. If Hartshorne and the other process thinkers were to regard their concept of God as *the* religious experience of God, then they would be guilty of the same fault that they sometimes accuse classical theists of having committed. An analogy, albeit a limited one, may be useful in clarifying my point.[3] A particular dress can accentuate the beauty of a model, drawing out her admirable features. Let us assume that there is no question here of hiding her less-than-presentable side nor of pretending that that she is more beautiful than she really is. Let us, for the sake of argument, accept that she *is* beautiful. Sometimes one particular dress will "do her justice" or "really suit her" while another, although it may be more expensive, fashionable or elegant, does not. Care regarding her dress is called for because the beauty of the model can be lost simply because the dress chosen was not the most appropriate. The criterion here is the model's beauty; one judges the dress with that criterion in mind. The dress is not what really makes the model beautiful, it merely highlights it. In similar fashion, the philosophical expression of an experience is not the experience, but it can articulate our basic insights more satisfactorily. Process thought is just one of many philosophical expressions of our religious experience of God.

Secondly, Hartshorne's concept of God has to be evaluated for its adequacy as well as for its meaningfulness as an articulation of what God is held to be religiously. Thus, it is not only the relevance nor the consistency of this way of thinking that requires scrutiny. If the process concept of God is intended to be another framework for understanding the believers' concrete experience of God, then believers will have to judge for themselves whether they find in process thought a fuller and more faithful representation of their basic insights compared to, say, classical theism. Hartshorne's stress on God's changing reality has offended many even though there is sufficient evidence that it does not threaten the belief in God's steadfastness or complete reliability which is the main thrust of the religious claim that God is immutable. Such a reaction is to be expected since Hartshorne's position appears to clash with traditional views. Nonetheless, his writings deserve the attention which they are only now getting. His doctrine of God's dipolarity, despite some problematic areas, goes a long way in making sense of the seemingly contradictory claims of religion regarding God. It represents a significant attempt to clarify the religious idea of God. How far it corresponds with the believers' own experience remains to be seen.

NOTES

1. Listed in the bibliography are some of the responses.
2. For a criticism of this approach of process theology see James D. Spiceland, "Process Theology", in *One God in Trinity* edited by Peter Toon and James D. Spiceland (Westchester, Ill.: Cornerstone Books, 1980), pp. 133 – 157.
3. I am grateful to my wife for suggesting and illustrating this analogy.

POSTSCRIPT

by

CHARLES HARTSHORNE

In my lecturing in various countries and states of my country I have had few comparable surprises, and none more pleasant, than when I encountered Santiago Sia in Belgium a few years ago. Here was a man from the Far East (the Philippine Islands), a country with a Spanish Catholic background, who had read extensively and intelligently in my writings and reacted in a basically positive way to them. Dr. Sia has given my extensive writings careful consideration, and has also read many books and articles dealing with my and related forms of philosophy. He has made a resolute attempt to digest all this material and come to a reasonable estimate of its value and possible limitations. I regard Sia as one who well understands and explains, as in this book, and in some published (and some unpublished) writings has ably defended (with whatever reservations) my form of philosophical theology.

Reading his book, including his other writings in which he deals with various writers critical of my ideas, has stimulated me to restate certain points. For example, I am accused by some of characterizing God as completely passive. I could caricature this reaction as follows: Because I deny that God does (decides or determines) everything (or is in that sense omnipotent − a word I tend to avoid), therefore I am really implying that God decides nothing. This I am infinitely far from doing. ("Infinitely" is used here with a certain literalness, though the word has more than one good meaning.) Without giving all my reasons for saying this, I offer the following.

First, I say, as Whitehead in effect does, that the (approximate) orderliness of nature, without which there could be no world, no conceivable creatures, is divinely imposed, and that the valid laws of nature are "acts of God". With Whitehead, also, I hold the idea of an infinite succession of cosmic epochs, each with its distinctive laws. This succession has an infinite actual past and an infinite potential future. Without the act or acts of divine ordering there could be nothing whatever. And I hold that there must be something.

Secondly, I hold that creativity is the ultimate form of forms of which every actuality is an instance. Actualities are experiences; to experience is to perform a creative act. This act has a passive aspect, but as a whole it is an act. Its passivity is that it takes its objective content from previous acts — as, in remembering, we derive content from our past experiences and, in perceiving, from past actualities other than our own experiences. An experience is creative — of what? Most immediately, of itself. Using previous actualities it produces itself as a new actuality. "The many become one and are increased by one." An actuality is an emergent synthesis. Its activity is one of "prehending", taking into itself, as nascent unitary reality, already created actualities, which thereby become its data. This act does not produce or alter the already created actualities. Their acts have already been achieved.

In the system of ideas just sketched, passivity is nothing but an aspect of activity as utilizing previous cases of activity. The act of prehending as such is universal to creativity and to actuality. God's eminent actuality has its aspect of self-creativity and of utilizing antecedent cases of creativity. Mind is not, in this philosophy, Locke's featureless wax awaiting definite form from some solid object; it is a power to *create additional actualities* that to some extent — completely only in the eminent or divine case — enjoy the values of their predecessors. Divine creativity is unique in ways that can be expressed with a certain partial literalness. In it there is *complete preservation* of antecedent value; also there is no possibility of the termination, nor has there been or could there be a first coming to be, of the divine enjoyer of values; also, finally, any actuality utilized by divine prehension will itself have been made possible by antecedent divine prehensions.

According to Whitehead, God's ordering of the world is an active affair in which God presents to each creature its "initial" (or, as I incline to put it, its tentative and approximate) subjective aim. God does not create a natural law as a static thing like the stone tablets of Moses; rather, God "persuades" each creature to take its place in the cosmos, makes the divine version of cosmic orderliness seem relevant to *its* decisions. If we could easily imagine just how this is done, we would be more godlike than we presumably are. But I see nothing merely metaphorical or analogical in the requirements of universality (*every* creature is influenced by divine persuasion) and of unsurpassability (excellence *beyond possible rivalry*).

The *final* creation, in whatever sense there is such a thing, is not the world. As Niebuhr says, "the end of history is beyond history". Niebuhr is cautious about developing the implicit content of this assertion. For process theology the ultimate creation, level of achievement, or consummation, is the divine life itself as active synthesis of the creatures. This for me is the logical conclusion from the imperative: love God with all thy being. Not nearly all, all! To will oneself as contribution to the divine life is the positive meaning of serving God. Our value is what we contribute to God.

The denial that God, being strictly self-sufficient, can acquire additional value from us is for me as unacceptable as any proposal I know of in these matters. It is supposed to exalt God. I think it insults God. It implies that our endeavors are not really "for God's sake", but only for the sake of us and other creatures. If God has all possible value once for all, only creaturely values can be enhanced. This makes God irrelevant. There is then no point in asking, "How can we serve God?" Here I feel, as Luther did in a different context, "I can do no other" than reject this. It seems nonsense to me.

As Dr. Sia explains, I argue that the notion of having all possible value, fully actualized, neglects the absurd consequences, additional to the one already mentioned, that follow. It implies, among other things, that our very clear intuition into the reality of incompatible values is to be discarded. What is to take its place has not, I charge, ever been made intelligible. In all artistic creation we find that every step we take toward making a beautiful whole excludes other possibilities that are also good. Positive values always conflict with some other positive values. Red here now excludes green here now. There is no one best possible color, best possible shape, or best possible arrangement of colors and shapes. Leibniz's best possible world got him into the contradiction that only a defectively wise God would choose any other possibility than the best. Hence since God's existence is necessary, as are his goodness and wisdom, there is really *only one* possible world. And God's act of creating would be wholly necessary and unfree. All Leibniz's genius could not conceal the absurdity.

How far can philosophy give rational support to the religious idea of divine love for the creatures? My view here is based on a doctrine which I accept fully from Whitehead (it agrees with a vaguer conviction that I had acquired from other sources) of "prehension" as the basic, universal form of experiencing and the most concrete mode of relationship by which the world hangs together as a cosmos. To experience is to prehend something, or in some sense *have it as a given*. This does not mean, intend or regard something as given, or believe in it as given; it means to possess it, whatever we believe about it. That it is given is the dual fact: it was already, independently, actualized, but a new actuality, our own, has now taken it into its own life. I use also the word intuition for this, though there are disadvantages in doing so.

Whitehead spells out the minimal, most universal import of prehending with the word *feeling*. This includes sensation. If what is prehended is concrete, there is prehension, hence feeling, on the side of the given as well as on the side of the actuality to which it is given. Therefore prehending, apart from abstract forms of objectivity, is always "feeling of feeling". The second occurrence of the word refers to one or more independent actualities and *their* feelings. So feeling of other's feeling(s) is a universal aspect of experiencing and, in this psychicalistic philosophy, of actuality. Now my proposition is: this basic meaning of prehending is also an essential aspect of "love". Sympathy, emotional participation in the life of another, is the least we should require for the application of this word. Accordingly, if God prehends creatures, God feels the feelings of creatures. If God does not do this, then according to this philosophy God does not experience or know the creatures, and love is one of the least appropriate words to characterize deity. If, however, God feels the creatures' feelings, and does so in eminent fashion, that is what I mean by saying that God loves the creatures. God wishes for the creatures what they, when they understand themselves, wish for themselves; for God participates in their longings, *cares* about their needs. To the divine life, we contribute the intrinsic beauty of our life, and all life is in principle beautiful. God shares our joys and sorrows with a participatory capacity for which ours offers only a faint analogy. Jesus, as we have his portrait in the Gospels, offers a sublime symbol for the idea. But in my philosophy there is no philosophically attractive alternative.

Our lives consist, minimally at least, of feelings; God is said to know everything. How does one know the feelings of others? No mere concept of feeling is my feeling or yours now. No command of mere concepts can duplicate or fully describe concrete feelings. I have often wondered what theologians thought they meant by speaking of God as one "to whom all hearts are open". Whitehead is the first great philosopher or theologian to tell us positively what this formula could mean. The medieval theologians told us with great clarity what it could not mean. We are in their debt for this. We know far better than we otherwise could that another way must be taken.

With Heidegger as well as Peirce, Whitehead, and many others I hold that all our best thought is anthropomorphic in the sense that we must take our own reality as sample of reality in general – the sample we most surely and adequately know. We know this sample not only by seeing, hearing, touching, tasting, smelling it as we can non-human things, but by being it. If we cannot generalize by analogy from this sample we cannot understand other things. Even physicists do this generalizing; for they posit an analogy between certain generalized patterns of thought in their minds and patterns in the cosmos at large. What they do not analogically generalize and extend to the non-human is patterns of feeling. They have reasons for not doing this, but there is a price for restricting ourselves entirely to this intellectual mode of analogy. It is part of the business of philosophy to see what can be done to find a place for feelings, that is, *values, qualities,* as well as mere causal, spatio-temporal *structures* (*quantities* and geometrical *orders*) in reality. Materialists and dualists do this at best only verbally.

Common sense tells us that animals are like us in having feelings (including sensations); plants and the minerals are a mystery for common sense, and for most philosophers if they are candid with themselves. Leibniz pointed the way to the only positive solution. *What acts as one feels as one* is the clue. An animal does this; does a plant? A cloud? A mountain, planet, or star? Science tends to support a negative answer to these questions. Apart from animals, what acts as one is invisible; in plants it is cells, in clouds and stars molecules. Of the active agents in nature only animals are visible one by one. Eventually Tom, Dick, Mary, and Helen may come to see what Leibniz saw three centuries ago. A cell is, in its active unity, far more like one of us than is a tree or a star. A cell really does things. And so does a molecule. Its acting may then involve feeling, though of course not human feeling. Even an ape does not have that. The language of feeling is not literal but analogical.

Most philosophers and theologians tend to omit one of the two chief modes of analogy between the human and the non-human.[1] As a parent is to a child, a ruler to a subject or citizen, a teacher to a pupil, so in eminent fashion is God to one of us. This analogy was basic in Hebrew thought. Greek thought used and abused the analogy in its polytheism. But Plato introduced another divine-human analogy, based on the relation of the mind (or soul) to its body. Aristotle, followed by the Church Fathers, dropped this analogy. In modern terms, it runs: as I (as active, sentient individual) am to my cells, especially my nerve cells, so, in eminent fashion, is God to the creatures. This analogy is helpful just where the interpersonal analogy is not. Parent and child (after infancy) are both human persons, incomparably more nearly equal than God and a human being. They are also less intimately united than God and creature. "Closer is [God] than breathing and nearer than hand or foot."

Consider now the trouble some have had with my statement that the divine prehension embraces all actualities and *in that sense* is all-inclusive. Do I as conscious individual include my body? Am I identical with my body? I venture to say that the critics have not thought out a clear answer to these questions. If not, then why should they be clear about the divine relation to the creatures? Suppose I felt all the feelings of my cells vividly and with ideal sympathy. Would my cells then be simply "outside" my awareness? What is "feeling of X" without X? Is God's feeling one thing, and our feeling simply another thing outside it? How then does God infallibly know our feeling? Of course two human persons are spatially outside one another. But the physicists and many philosophers view the world as far more intimately unified than raw common sense finds it. Quantum physics is relevant here. Moreover, the divine self is unique in being ubiquitous and its awareness is all-embracing.

Is God simply the cosmos of creatures? No more than I am simply my cells and molecules. Indeed, God is incomparably farther from mere identity with the cosmic or divine body than I am with my body. In dreamless sleep what am I in addition to a living body? The divine consciousness is not conceived as intermittent. Do we create our bodies? To a certain extent yes, according to some scientists with whom I am glad to agree. Alas, many of us create rather poor bodies, even though we were born with good ones. I am speaking not only of the physical effects of bad or foolish physical behaviors but of psychosomatic phenomena, whose extent we only now partially and vaguely begin to know and honestly take into account. God is defined as incapable of bad behavior and the divine body cannot be worsened by divine action. Its "cells" can cause each other suffering, but divine suffering is vicarious and is not divine ill-health, or in the least a threat of divine death. It is interesting that Whitehead in one passage rejects, and never affirms, the mind-body analogy. I find his reasons for this weak. But the late philosophical theologian D.C. McIntosh did affirm it, as did the German theologian Pfleiderer.[2] They were both distinguished writers in their time. In talking to McIntosh I felt there was in him a rare combination of intellectual integrity and generosity toward the thought of others.

The divine body is not merely our cosmos from the big bang to the present. That is only the body of the present cosmic epoch. For "divine time" (Berdyaev uses this expression and Whitehead − somewhat inconsistently − and K. Barth imply it) the past is fully real in the divine present. God loses nothing once acquired. And God could have been God though every past phase of the divine body had been different. That God must have a body does not mean that there is some body that God must have. Divine power guarantees whatever divine existence requires. But what an individual existence requires is not all that an individual's actuality can enjoy or profit by. What one "needs" in the strict sense is not all that one can profit by. This, I assert, should be applied, *eminenter*, to deity. We can profit God without making God depend in the least for very existence upon us.

I wish to emphasize that my conclusions are supported by some definite methodological principles. Consider, for instance, the question of "pantheism". I have shown that historical pantheism, as in the Stoics and Spinoza, is only one of nine mathematically possible theoretical options in conceiving God, using the concepts necessary and contingent.[3] My view is another of these nine, in several basic ways widely different from what I call pantheism, and comparably different from classical theism, as in the Middle Ages. This classical option is a third of the nine. Aristotelian theism is a fourth. The distinctions and historical identifications are, I claim, quite definite and clear. There remain five other options. I propose rules for elimination of options as incoherent (either contradictory or without clear meaning), rules that I claim are rational. Several involve a standard axiom of modal logic. Eight of the options are eliminated by two or more rules, leaving one option, my own, conforming to all the rules, except two supposed rules that I argue are specious, though they help to explain why my view (panentheism or dual transcendence) has been neglected.

Instead of necessity and contingency one can use various other universal contrasts, including absolute (or independent) and relative (or dependent), infinite and finite, simple and complex. Again there will be nine options, rational rules for elimination, and process theism will be supported by the rules.

I prefer dual transcendence to "dipolarity" (Whitehead) in this application, for I am serious about transcendence, which for me implies, surpasses all possible rivals. I also regard as essential the procedure of using mathematical structures (in this case the combinations of four concepts, giving 16 options, nine of which might be held to be positive ideas of God, and in that broad sense theistic.[4] The technical basis of my metaphysics is illustrated by the foregoing, partly strictly systematic and partly historical, mode of argument: exhaust the conceptual options, judge each option by rational rules of conceptual coherence.

The rules of elimination spoken of can of course be questioned. So can any assumptions taken for granted by the questioner. To speak of "intuition" in such matters (a different use of the word from the one mentioned above) is to recognize that not only do arguments have premises but also one cannot go through an infinite regress of arguments for premises of arguments. Unless something is admitted as reasonable without further argument, not much can be done by argument. We human beings must do the best we can with our capacity to grasp conceptual relations. At some point we trust our intuitions. Logicians as well as metaphysicians employ terms like "counterintuitive". Only divine intuitions are absolutely definitive – apart from trivial matters, as in finite arithmetic. To the complaint that appeal to intuition does not dispose of all disagreement, the answer is that argument does not do so either. Disagreement is scarcely to be overcome in metaphysics. We do what we can. But there is, I believe, a wide gap between mere arbitrary prejudice, in some cases become a tradition with great psychological power, and conviction arrived at in the light of a careful survey of theoretical possibilities (a requirement usually not met in metaphysics).

It may be replied that relations of concepts determine only what is consistent or inconsistent, but not what exists. I agree in large part with Aristotle, Peirce, and Whitehead, three logicians, in this matter. Whatever has a temporal beginning is contingent and only observation can tell us that it exists. Whatever has no temporal beginning is not contingent, even logically, if that term is given appropriate scope. The idea that there can be no concepts that necessarily have instances is itself a conceptual claim, and one that I hold is incoherent. The most *general* concepts by conceptual (that is logical) necessity must have instances. No particular observation is needed for this. Anything defined as without temporal beginning (as "God" is defined) is either impossible (not genuinely, coherently conceivable) or its non-existence is inconceivable and its existence necessary. Special observations are not to the point.

The foregoing does not mean that no experience is needed for metaphysical knowledge of eternal, necessary aspects of reality. Without experience there is nothing, no words, no meanings, no anything. All knowledge is "experiential". But not all legitimate claims to knowledge are conceivably falsifiable by observation. I employ Popper's definitions here in holding that metaphysical statements, though not meaningless, had best be termed "non-empirical"; though of course in thinking them we are using and having experiences. "Experiential" and "empirical" are not synonymous. Nor is the dogma that existential assertions (no matter how abstract, for example, "there is something"), are all contingent a valid axiom. "Total non-existence" is what no experience could illustrate or provide meaning for. That there "might be no being" is as absurd or contradictory as it sounds.

I have no doubt that some of the things I have said could be said better and that some of them will need to be unsaid. But I really cannot imagine that pre-process metaphysics, as in Aristotle, Anselm, Aquinas, Leibniz, Hegel (who could be called a cloudy, loose-thinking, proto-process metaphysician), Bradley, Royce, were as close to the truth as we can now come. Nor can I imagine that Hume, Kant, Russell, or Wittgenstein have simply demonstrated that all metaphysics must be (what I agree much metaphysics has partly been) misuse of words, linguistic confusion. To *define* metaphysics in this way is a peculiarly vicious, negative, "persuasive" definition.

If, as I hold (with Anselm, Descartes, and Leibniz) "God exists" makes no coherent sense taken as a contingent proposition, then atheism makes sense only if taken as meaning, "God's existence is impossible", not coherently conceivable.

In other words, atheism must claim to be a necessary truth. Anselm's principle does not suffice to rule out this option. I regard the ontological argument as only one of a number of arguments whose force taken together is stronger than any one by itself. I regret having called such arguments "proofs", as though each simply settled the question for all intelligent, honest, and trained minds. Little in philosophy can be proved in that sense. To make the limitations of the "proofs" or arguments more obvious I formulate each as a set of several options, decision among which is by elimination, somewhat as in the case of the nine forms of theism.[5] This is a new proposal, not yet evaluated by my colleagues, though a good dissertation on it by Don Viney has been published.[6]

I am a theist because there is no other doctrine on the same level of generality (God being conceived as the individual with strictly *universal* functions) that I can see as conceptually coherent; and my belief is rational at least to this extent that I have a definite logical way of exhausting the possible options (there are 15) other than my own. The role of strict logic is partly to show this exhaustiveness. In judging what conceptual combinations are or are not coherent a kind of "intellectual intuition" comes in. It, or an implicit claim to it, will also come in when atheists deal with the question. The claim to rationality is, I think, strengthened if one has some familiarity with historical examples of the theoretical options referred to. In the middle ages this familiarity was scarcely possible, and I hold was not acquired. Certainly Kant did not possess it in a degree remotely comparable to that which is now possible. If Wittgenstein had anything like this he concealed it well.

The question of immortality is beset with ambiguity. Divine process cannot terminate, God is indeed immortal. Surely, however, there must be a difference in principle between this and any human or other creaturely immortality. The process view is that there is a literal sense for our non-divine kind of indestructibility. Our careers, or "personally-ordered" sequential "societies of actualities", after infancy on a high level of animal consciousness, are temporally finite, each with a first and (when and after we die) a last member, but each career with its actualities is an "everlasting" possession of divine prehension. God creates in his conscious life a not conceivably surpassable retention of our lives as actually enjoyed. All that we have ever been is indestructibly real. As a book has a first and last chapter, and as the termination of the last chapter does not destroy the book, neither does death destroy our earthly actuality.

Even if our careers did extend beyond death in some form it would not follow that our posthumous futures would continue to prolong themselves infinitely. Infinity is not our attribute but God's.

Is justice done on earth, and if not, must it be done after death? Our legal justice is, as we more and more see, an all-too-human-affair. We should hesitate to exalt it analogically into a divine attribute. Rewarding and punishing are means not final ends. The end is happiness, life as beautiful, for creatures and Creator. Would trying to make Hitler as one individual suffer proportionately to his wicked causing of misery to millions be a constructive undertaking? I think it would make a miserable addition to a total reality that had absorbed sufficient misery at his hands already.

I see no incompatibility between divine love and divine justice in any sense in which the second expression makes sense. The laws of nature plus human (partly but genuinely free) contrivances almost guarantee that bad behavior will have some bad consequences for the individual and good behavior, some good consequences. Virtue is, to some extent and in some ways, its own reward and vice its own punishment. To guarantee more than this would mean a radical restricting of the freedom of individuals, with its implied element of chance and partial disorder, an element that could not be entirely absent from any conceivable heaven, and without which there could, according to the ultimacy, or absolute universality, of creativity, be neither good nor evil, indeed nothing at all. And there must be something. So I am unimpressed by the argument from justice as ground for deifying our natures to the extent of attributing prospective temporal infinity to ourselves. We are everlasting, though not eternal, and we are not even everlasting as God is. We are to love our neighbor as we love ourselves, but we are not to love either self or neighbor as we love God. The ancient Jews understood some of this. Not creaturely enjoyment of God is the final value but (analogically expressed) God's enjoyment of creaturely enjoyment. There are aesthetic objections to an infinite career for an individual creature. It would be either infinite monotony, as some have remarked, or the capacity to assimilate infinite variety that is one definition of deity. As Robert Frost put it, "Earth's the right place for love/ I don't know where it's likely to go better."

I once had the privilege of talking with Reinhold Niebuhr about all this. He said that the Whiteheadian "objective immortality" in God as "consequent" *might* be the religious truth. But he preferred to leave the matter as a mystery not to be penetrated by rational speculation. Niebuhr's one published reference to me was definitely positive. He was the greatest preacher in my experience.

If a philosophy is to become important it must be interpreted by writers with a variety of backgrounds. Dr. Sia's is certainly different from that of most interpreters of my or Whitehead's thought. My own early religious experience was entirely Protestant and my knowledge of foreign philosophers and theologians has been chiefly continental or Asiatic – or of English thinkers before, or early in, this century – whereas Dr. Sia has been dealing mainly with Filipino, African, Irish and English students and teachers of the present day, particularly those with Catholic perspectives. My philosophical theology has been tolerably understood by Protestants of many varieties, Catholics of several countries, Unitarian-Universalists, Rabbis, some Hindus, Chinese, and still others. The time may even come when the country that, with supplementary help from my country, produced the greatest metaphysician of this century, will begin to understand the importance for religion of the type of theism of which Whitehead is the most famous, but far from the only, representative. (Berdyaev is another and independent one.) Dr. Sia's carefully researched work should help to hasten that day.

NOTES

1. For the soul-body analogy see PSG, pp. 251 (2nd column) to 253; DR, pp. 69 and 110 – 11; LP, pp. 191 – 214; NTOT, pp. 98 – 100; CSPM, pp. 266 and 271; IOGT, pp. 251 and 278 – 79; OOTM, pp. 52 – 56 and 59.
2. PSG, p. 270, sec. 367. Note also sec. 366.
3. CSPM, p. 266.
4. CSPM, pp. 266 and 271.
5. *Ibid.*, pp. 281 and 286.
6. Donald Wayne Viney, *Charles Hartshorne's Global Argument for God's Existence: Analysis and Assessment*. Albany: State University of New York Press, 1984.

SELECTED BIBLIOGRAPHY

A complete list of Charles Hartshorne's writings, arranged chronologically, was compiled and published by his wife, Dorothy. The bibliography of his writings until 1976 appeared in *Process Studies*, VI, 1 (Spring, 1976), pp. 73 – 93. The up-dated list, which includes his writings up to 1980, was published in *Process Studies*, XI, 2 (Summer, 1981), pp. 108 – 112. Bibliographies of secondary sources, also compiled by Mrs. Hartshorne, will be found in *Process Studies*, III, 3 (Fall, 1973), pp. 179 – 227 and *Process Studies*, XI, 2 (Spring, 1981), pp. 112 – 120. A list of dissertations and theses on Charles Hartshorne was prepared by Dean R. Fowler and published in *Process Studies*, III, 4 (Winter, 1973), pp. 304 – 307. Addenda to that list, compiled by Philip Ricards, appeared in *Process Studies* XI, 2 (Summer, 1981), pp. 151 – 152.

PRIMARY SOURCES

Books

Anselm's Discovery. La Salle: Open Court, 1967.
Aquinas to Whitehead: Seven Centuries of Metaphysics of Religion. The Aquinas Lecture, 1976. Milwaukee: Marquette University Publications, 1976.
Beyond Humanism: Essays in the New Philosophy of Nature. Chicago: Willett, Clark & Co., 1937. Bison Book Edition, with new Preface. Lincoln: The University of Nebraska Press, 1968.
Creative Synthesis and Philosophic Method. London: SCM Press, Ltd., 1970. La Salle: Open Court, 1970.
Creativity in American Philosophy. State University of New York Press, 1984.
The Divine Relativity: A Social Conception of God. The Terry Lectures, 1947. New Haven: Yale University Press, 1948.
Insights and Oversights of Great Thinkers: an Evaluation of Western Philosophy. State University of New York Press, 1983.
The Logic of Perfection and Other Essays in Neoclassical Metaphysics. La Salle: Open Court, 1962.
Man's Vision of God and the Logic of Theism. Chicago: Willett, Clark & Co., 1941. N.Y.: Harper and Brothers Publishers, 1948. Reprinted, 1964, by Archon Books, Hamden, Conn.

A Natural Theology for Our Time. La Salle: Open Court, 1967.

Omnipotence and Other Theological Mistakes. State University of New York Press, 1984.

Philosophers Speak of God (With William L. Reese). Chicago: The University of Chicago Press, 1953. Reissued in 1976 in Midway Reprints.

The Philosophy and Psychology of Sensation. Chicago: The University of Chicago Press, 1934. Reissued in 1968 by Kennikat Press.

Reality as Social Process: Studies in Metaphysics and Religion. Glencoe: The Free Press and Boston: The Beacon Press, 1953. Reprinted by Hafner, 1971.

The Social Conception of the Universe [3 chapters from RSP] edited by Keiji Matsunobu. Tokyo: Aoyama, and N.Y.: Macmillan, 1967.

Whitehead and the Modern World: Science, Metaphysics, and Civilization, Three Essays on the Thought of Alfred North Whitehead. By Victor Lowe, Charles Hartshorne, and A.H. Johnson. "Whitehead's Metaphysics" by C. Hartshorne, 25 – 41. Boston: The Beacon Press, 1950. Reprinted by Books for Libraries Press, 1972.

Whitehead's Philosophy: Selected Essays, 1935 – 1970. Lincoln: University of Nebraska Press, 1972.

Whitehead's View of Reality (With Creighton Peden). N.Y.: The Pilgrim Press, 1981.

Collected Papers of Charles Sanders Peirce, Vols I – VI. Edited by Charles Hartshorne and Paul Weiss. Cambridge: Harvard University Press, 1931 – 1935.

Articles

"Absolute Objects and Relative Subjects: a Reply to F.H. Parker", *Review of Metaphysics*, XV, 1 (Sept., 1961), 174 – 188.

"Abstract and Concrete Approaches to Deity", *Union Seminary Quarterly Review*, XX, 3 (March, 1965), 265 – 270.

"Abstract and Concrete in God: a Reply to Julian Hartt", *Review of Metaphysics*, XVII, 2 (Dec., 1963), 289 – 295.

"The Acceptance of Death", *Philosophical Aspects of Thanatology*, Vol. I, eds. Florence M. Hetzler and Austin H. Kutscher. N.Y.: MSS Information Corporation, 1978, 83 – 87.

"Analysis and Cultural Lag in Philosophy", *Southern Journal of Philosophy*, XI, 2 – 3 (Spring and Summer, 1973), 105 – 112.

"Alternative Conceptions of God", [from MV] *Religious Belief and Philosophical Thought*, ed. William P. Alston. N.Y.: Harcout, Brace & World, 1963, 320 – 337.

"Anthropomorphic Tendencies in Positivism", *Philosophy of Science*, VIII, 2 (April, 1941), 184–203.

"Are Religious Dogmas Cognitive and Meaningful?", *Journal of Philosophy*, LI, 5 (March 4, 1954), 148–150.

"Are There Absolutely Specific Universals?", *Journal of Philosophy*, LXVIII, 3 (Feb. 11, 1971), 76–78.

"Being and Becoming: Review of Harold N. Lee, *Percepts, Concepts and Theoretic Knowledge*", *Review of Books and Religion*, II, 9 (Mid-June, 1973), 7.

"Bell's Theorem and Stapp's Revised View of Space-Time", *Process Studies*, VII, 3 (Fall, 1977), 183–191.

"Beyond Enlightened Self-Interest: a Metaphysics of Ethics", *Ethics*, LXXXIV, 3 (April, 1974), 201–216. Reprinted in *Religious Experience and Process Theology*, eds. Harry James Cargas and Bernard Lee. N.Y.: Paulist Press, 1976, 301–322.

"Biology and the Spiritual View of the World: a Comment on Dr Birch's Paper", *Christian Scholar*, XXXVII, 3 (Sept., 1954), 408–409.

"The Buddhist-Whiteheadian View of the Self and the Religious Traditions", *Proceedings of the 9th International Congress for the History of Religions*. Tokyo and Kyoto, 1958. Tokyo: Maruzen, 1960, 298–302.

"Can Man Transcend His Animality?", *Monist*, LV, 2 (April, 1971), 208–217.

"Can There Be Proofs for the Existence of God?", *Religious Language and Knowledge*, eds. Robert H. Ayers and William T. Blackstone. Athens: University of Georgia Press, 1972, 62–75.

"Can We Understand God?", *Louvain Studies*, VII, 2 (Fall, 1978), 75–84.

"The Case for Idealism", *Philosophical Forum*, I, 1, n.s. (Fall, 1968), 7–23.

"Categories, Transcendentals, and Creative Experiencing", *The Monist*, LXVI, 3 (July, 1983), 319–335.

"Causal Necessities: an Alternative to Hume", *Philosophical Review*, XLIII, 4 (Oct., 1954), 479–499.

"The Centrality of Reason in Philosophy (Replies to Questions for Charles Hartshorne)", *Philosophy in Context*, Suppl. to Vol. 4 (1975), 5–11.

"Chance, Love, and Incompatibility", Presidential Address, Western Division of the American Philosophical Association Meeting at Columbus, Ohio, April 29, 1949, *Philosophical Review*, LVIII, 5 (Sept., 1949), 429–450.

"Charles Peirce and Quantum Mechanics", *Transactions of the Charles S. Peirce Society*, LX, 4 (Fall, 1973), 191–201.

"Comment" in *The Creative Advance* by Eugene H. Peters. St. Louis: Bethany Press, 1966, 133–143.

"Comments on Stallknecht's Theses", *Review of Metaphysics*, IX, 3 (1956), 464 – 465.

"The Compound Individual", *Philosophical Essays for Alfred North Whitehead*, ed. Otis H. Lee. N.Y.: Longmans Green, 1936, 193 – 220.

"Concerning Abortion: an Attempt at a Rational View", *The Christian Century*, XCVIII, 2 (Jan. 21, 1981), 42 – 45. Reprinted in *Speak Out Against the New Right*, ed. H.V. Vetter. Boston: The Beacon Press, 1982, 152 – 157.

"Contingency and the New Era in Metaphysics, I", *Journal of Philosophy*, XXIX, 16 (Aug. 4, 1932), 421 – 431; "II", *Ibid.*, XXIX, 17 (Aug. 18, 1932), 457 – 469.

"A Conversation with Charles Hartshorne at Hiram College", ed. Eugene Peters, *Eclectic: a Journal of Ideas*, I, 1 (Winter, 1972), 1 – 18.

"Could There Have Been Nothing? a Reply to Craighead", *Process Studies*, I, 1 (Spring, 1971), 25 – 28.

"Creativity and the Deductive Logic of Causality", *Review of Metaphysics*, XXVII, 1 (Sept., 1973), 62 – 74.

"Criteria for Ideas of God", *Insight and Vision: Essays in Philosophy in Honor of Radoslav Andrea Tsanoff*, ed. Konstantin Kolenda, *Rice University Studies*, LI, 4 (Fall, 1965), 85 – 95; San Antonio: Principia Press of Trinity University, 1966, 85 – 95.

"A Critique of Peirce's Idea of God", in "Abstracts of Papers to be Read at the Joint Meeting of the Eastern and Western Divisions of the American Philosophical Association, Columbia University, Dec., 1939", *Journal of Philosophy*, XXXVI, 25 (Dec. 7, 1939), 683 – 684.

"Deity as the Inclusive Transcendence", *Evolution in Perspective: Commentaries in Honor of Pierre Lecomte du Noüy*, eds. George N. Schuster and Ralph E. Thorson. Notre Dame and London: University of Notre Dame Press, 1970, 155 – 160.

"Deliberation and Excluded Middle", *Journal of Philosophy*, LXI, 16 (Sept. 3, 1964), 476 – 477.

"Determinism, Memory, and the Metaphysics of Becoming", *Pacific Philosophy Forum*, IV, 4 (May, 1965), 81 – 85.

"The Development of My Philosophy", *Contemporary American Philosophy: Second Series*, ed. John E. Smith. London: Allen & Unwin, 1970, 211 – 228.

"The Development of Process Philosophy", [from the introduction to *Philosophers of Process*, ed. Douglas Browning. N.Y.: Random House, 1965, v – vii] *Process Theology: Basic Writings*, ed. Ewert H. Cousins. N.Y.: Newman Press, 1971, 47 – 61.

"The Dipolar Conception of Deity", *Review of Metaphysics*, XXI, 2 (Dec., 1967), 273 – 289.

"Divine Absoluteness and Divine Relativity", *Transcendence*, eds. Herbert W. Richardson and Donald R. Cutler. Boston: Beacon Press, 1969, 164 – 171.

"The Divine Relativity and Absoluteness: a Reply to John Wild", *Review of Metaphysics*, IV, 1 (Sept., 1950), 31 – 60.

"Duality versus Dualism and Monism", *Japanese Religions*, V, 1 (April, 1969), 51 – 63.

"Efficient Causality in Aristotle and St. Thomas: a Review Article", [of Francis X. Meehan's book. Washington: Catholic University Press, 1940], *Journal of Religion*, XXV, 1 (Jan., 1945), 25 – 32.

"El valor como disfrute del contraste y la teoría acumulativa del proceso", tr. J.L. González, *Dianoia, Anuario de Filosofía*, X (1964), 182 – 194.

" "Emptiness" and Fullness in Asiatic and Western Thought", *Journal of Chinese Philosophy*, VI (1979), 411 – 420.

Entries, *An Encyclopedia of Religion*, ed. Vergilius Ferm, N.Y.: Philosophical Library, 1945. Acosmism; analogy; anthropomorphism; anthropopathism; Aristotle and Aristotelianism; axiom; Berkeley, George; Carneades; cause; Copernican astronomy; eternal; eternity; ether; etiology, aetiology; foreknowledge, Divine; Gerson, Levi Ben; God, as personal; Hume; infinite; Kant, Immanuel; omnipotence; omnipresence; omniscience; panentheism; panlogism; pantheism; Peirce, Charles Sanders; perfect, perfection; Ptolemaic astronomy; Renovier, Charles; Spencer, Herbert; Spinoza, Benedict; time; transcendence; Whitehead, Alfred North.

"The Environmental Results of Technology", *Philosophy and Environmental Crisis*, ed. William T. Blackstone. Athens: University of Georgia Press, 1974, 69 – 78.

"Equalitarianism and the Great Inequalities", *Emory Alumnus* XXXVI, 7 (Nov., 1960), 24 – 25, 49.

"Equality, Freedom and the Insufficiency of Empiricism", *Southwestern Journal of Philosophy*, I, 3 (Fall, 1970), 20 – 27.

"Eternity", "Absolute", "God", *Prophetic Voices: Ideas and Words on Revolution*, ed. Ned O'Gorman. N.Y.: Random House, 1969; N.Y.: Vintage Books, 1970, 130 – 148.

"Ethics and the New Theology", *International Journal of Ethics*, XLV, 1 (Oct., 1934), 90 – 101.

"Ethics and the Process of Living", *Man and His Conduct: Philosophical Essays in Honor of Risieri Frondizi*, ed. Jorge J.E. Rio Piedras Gracia. Porto Rico: Editorial Universitaria, 1980, 191 – 202.

"Ethics of Contributionism", *Responsibilities to Future Generations*, ed. Ernest Patridge. Buffalo, N.Y.: Prometheus Books, 1981, 103 – 108.

"Existential Propositions and the Law of Categories", *Fascicule 1, Proceedings of the 10th International Congress of Philosophy*, ed. E.W. Beth et al. Amsterdam: North-Holland Publishing Co., 1948, 342 – 344.

"Foreword", *The Ontological Argument of Charles Hartshorne* by George L. Missoula Goodwin. Montana: Scholars Press, 1978, xi – xviii.

"The Formal Validity and Real Significance of the Ontological Argument", *Philosophical Review*, LIII, 3 (May, 1944), 225 – 245.

"Foundations for a Humane Ethics: What Human Beings Have in Common with Other Higher Animals", *On the Fifth Day: Animal Rights and Human Ethics*, eds. Richard Knowles Morris and Michael W. Fox. Washington, D.C.: Acropolis Books, Ltd., 1978, 154 – 172.

"Four Principles of Method – with Applications", *Monist*, XLIII, 1 (Jan., 1933), 40 – 72.

"Freedom, Individuality, and Beauty in Nature", *Snowy Egret*, XXIV, 2 (Autumn, 1960), 5 – 14.

"Freedom Requires Indeterminism and Universal Causality", *Journal of Philosophy*, LV, 19 (Sept. 11, 1958), 793 – 811.

"From Colonial Beginnings to Philosophical Greatness", *Monist*, XLVIII, 3 (July, 1964), 317 – 331.

"Further Fascination of the Ontological Argument: Replies to Richardson", *Union Seminary Quarterly Review*, XVIII, 3, Part I (March, 1963), 244 – 245.

"God and Man not Rivals", *Journal of Liberal Religion*, VI, 2 (Autumn, 1944), 9 – 13.

"God and the Social Structure of Reality", and "Answers to Questions", *Theology in Crisis: A Colloquium on "The Credibility of God"*. New Concord, Ohio: Muskingum College, 1967, 19 – 32, 44 – 50.

"God as Absolute, Yet Related to All", *Review of Metaphysics*, I, 1 (Sept., 1947), 24 – 51.

"God as the Supreme Relativity", *Japanese Religions*, IV, 1 (Dec., 1964), 30 – 33.

"The God of Religion and the God of Philosophy", *Talk of God: Royal Institute of Philosophy Lectures, Vol. II – 1967 – 68*. London: Macmillan, 1969, 152 – 167.

"God in General Philosophical Thought", *The Encyclopedia Hebraica*, III, 1951 (Jewish Calendar 5711). Jerusalem: Encyclopedia Publishing Co., 1951, 467 – 478.

"God's Existence: a Conceptual Problem", *Religious Experience and Truth: a Symposium*, ed. Sidney Hook. N.Y.: University Press, 1961, 211 – 219.

"Grounds for Believing in God's Existence", *Meaning, Truth and God*, ed.

L.S. Rouner. Notre Dame and London: University of Notre Dame Press, 1982, 17 – 33.

"How Some Speak and Yet Do Not Speak of God", *Philosophy and Phenomenological Research*, XXIII, 2 (Dec., 1962), 274 – 276.

"Hume's Metaphysics and its Present-Day Influence", *New Scholasticism*, XXXV, 2 (April, 1961), 152 – 171.

"Husserl and the Social Structure of Immediacy", *Philosophical Essays in Memory of Edmund Husserl*, ed. Marvin Faber. Cambridge: Harvard University Press, 1940, 219 – 230.

"The Idea of a Worshipful Being", *Southern Journal of Philosophy*, II, 4 (Winter, 1964), 165 – 167.

"The Idea of Creation", *Review of Metaphysics*, IX, 3 (March, 1956), 464 – 465.

"The Idea of Creativity in American Philosophy", *Journal of Karnatak University* [India]: *Social Sciences* II, 1966, 1 – 13.

"The Idea of God – Literal or Analogical?", *Christian Scholar*, XXIX, 2 (June, 1956), 131 – 136.

"Ideal Knowledge Defines Reality: What was True in Idealism", *Journal of Philosophy*, XLIII, 21 (Oct. 10, 1946), 573 – 582.

"Idealism and Our Experience of Nature", *Philosophy, Religion and the Coming World Civilization: Essays in Honor of William Ernest Hocking*, ed. Leroy S. Rouner. The Hague: Martinus Nijhoff, 1966, 70 – 80.

"The Immortality of the Past: Critique of a Prevalent Misinterpretation", *Review of Metaphysics*, VII, 1 (Sept., 1953), 98 – 112.

"In Defense of Wordsworth's View of Nature", *Philosophy and Literature*, IV, 1 (Spring, 1980), 80 – 91.

"Individual Differences and the Ideal of Equality", *New South*, XVIII, 2 (Feb., 1963), 3 – 8.

"The Individual is a Society", *The Individual and Society: Essays Presented to David L. Miller on his 75th Birthday,* ed. Michael P. Jones et al. Norman, Oklahoma: Southwestern Journal of Philosophy, 1978, 73 – 88.

"Interrogations of Charles Hartshorne: Replies", conducted by William Alston. *Philosophical Interrogations*, eds. Sydney and Beatrice Rome. N.Y.: Holt, Rinehart and Winston, 1964, 321 – 354.

"Introduction to Second Edition", *Saint Anselm: Basic Writings*, tr. S.W. Deane. La Salle: Open Court, 1962, 1 – 19.

"Is God's Existence a State of Affairs?", *Faith and the Philosophers*, ed. John Hick. N.Y.: St. Martin's Press, 1964, 26 – 33.

"Is the Denial of Existence Ever Contradictory?", *Journal of Philosophy*, LXIII, 4 (Feb. 17, 1966), 85 – 93.

"Is Whitehead's God the God of Religion?", *Ethics*, LIII, 3 (April, 1943), 219–227.

"John Hick on Logical and Ontological Necessity", *Religious Studies*, XIII, 2 (1977), 155–165.

"John Wisdom on "Gods": Two Views of the Logic of Theism", *Downside Review* (Winter, 1958–59), 5–17.

"Kant's Refutation Still Not Convincing; A Reply", *Monist*, LII, 2 (April, 1968), 312–316.

"The Kinds of Theism: a Reply", *Journal of Religion*, XXXIV, 2 (April, 1954), 127–131.

"La Creatividad Participada", tr. Sira Jaén, *Revista de Filosofia de la Universidad de Costa Rica*, III, 11 (Jan.–June, 1962), 237–244.

"La Philosophie de la religion aux Etats-Unis", *Les Etudes Philosophiques*, VII, 1–2 (Jan.–June, 1952), 50–56.

"Leibniz's Greatest Discovery", *Journal of the History of Ideas*, VII, 4 (Oct., 1946), 411–421.

"The Logic of the Ontological Argument", *Journal of Philosophy*, LVIII, 17 (Aug. 17, 1961), 471–473.

"The Logical Structure of Givenness", *Philosophical Quarterly* VIII, 33 (Oct., 1958), 307–316.

"Love and Dual Transcendence", *Union Seminary Quarterly Review*, XXX, 2–4 (Winter–Summer, 1975), 94–100.

"Man in Nature", *Experience, Existence, and the Good: Essays in Honor of Paul Weiss*, ed. Irwin C. Lieb. Carbondale: Southern Illinois University Press, 1961, 89–99.

"Man's Fragmentariness", *Wesleyan Studies in Religion*, XLI, 6 (1963–64), 17–28.

"A Mathematical Analysis of Theism", *Review of Religion*, VIII, 1 (Nov., 1943), 20–38.

"The Meaning of "Is Going to Be"", *Mind*, LXXIV, 293 (Jan., 1965), 46–58.

"Metaphysical Statements as Nonrestrictive and Existential", *Review of Metaphysics*, XII, 1 (Sept., 1958), 35–47.

"Metaphysics and the Modality of Existential Judgments", *The Relevance of Whitehead: Philosophical Essays in Commemoration of the Centenary of the Birth of A.N. Whitehead*, ed. Ivor Leclerc. London: Allen and Unwin, 1961, 107–121.

"Metaphysics Contributes to Ornithology", *Theoria to Theory*, XIII, 2 (1972), 127–140.

"Metaphysics for Positivists", *Philosophy of Science*, II, 3 (July, 1935), 287–303.

"A Metaphysics of Individualism", *Innocence and Power*, ed. Gordon Mills. Austin: University of Texas Press, 1965, 131 – 146.

"Metaphysics in North America", *Contemporary Philosophy: A Survey*, ed. Raymond Klibansky. Florence: La Nuova Italia Editrice, 1969, 36 – 49.

"Mind, Matter, and Freedom", *Scientific Monthly*, LXXVIII, 5 (May 1954), 314 – 320.

"Mind and Matter in Ryle, Ayers, and C.I. Lewis", *Idealistic Studies*, I, 1 (Jan., 1971), 13 – 32.

"Mind as Memory and Creative Love", *Theories of the Mind*, ed. Jordan M. Scher. N.Y.: The Fress Press of Glencoe, 1962, 440 – 463.

"The Modern World and a Modern View of God", *Crane Review*, IV, 2 (Winter, 1962), 73 – 85.

"My Neoclassical Metaphysics", *Tijdschrift voor Philosophie*, XLII, 1 (March, 1980), 3 – 10.

"Mysticism and Rationalistic Metaphysics", *Monist*, LIX, 4 (Oct., 1976), 463 – 469.

"The Nature of Philosophy", *Philosophy in Context: An Experiment in Teaching*, Vol. 4, ed. Leslie Armour. Cleveland: Cleveland State University, 1975, 7 – 16.

"Necessity", *Review of Metaphysics*, XXI, 2 (Dec., 1967), 290 – 296.

"The Neglect of Relative Predicates in Modern Philosophy", *American Philosophical Quarterly*, XIV, 4 (Oct., 1977), 309 – 318.

"A New Look at the Problem of Evil", *Current Philosophical Issues: Essays in Honor of Curt John Ducasse*, comp. and ed. Frederick C. Dommeyer. Springfield, Ill.: Charles C. Thomas, 1966, 201 – 212.

"The New Metaphysics and Current Problems, I", *New Frontier*, I, 1 (Sept., 1934), 24 – 31; "II" *Ibid.*, I, 5 (Nov. – Dec., 1934), 8 – 14.

"The New Pantheism – I", *Christian Register*, CXV, 8 (Feb. 20, 1936), 119 – 120; "II" *Ibid.*, CXV, 9 (Feb. 27, 1936), 141 – 143.

"A New Philosophic Conception of the Universe", *Hibbert Journal*, XLIV, 1 (Oct., 1945), 14 – 21.

"New Propositions and New Truths", *Review of Metaphysics*, IX, 4 (June, 1956), 656 – 661.

"A New World and a New World View", *The Life of Choice*, ed. Clark Kucheman. Boston: Beacon Press, 1978, 82 – 92.

"Noch einmal die Zufälligkeit der Welt und Notwendigkeit Gottes: Erwiderung an Dr Ferdinand Bergenthal", *Philosophisches Jahrbuch*, LIX, 2 (1949), 355 – 356.

"Ob Göttliches Wissen um die weltliche Existenz notwendig sein kann: eine Erwiderung", *Ibid.*, LX, 4 (1950), 469 – 471.

134

"Obligability and Determinism", *Journal of Social Philosophy*, II, 2 (Oct., 1971), 1 – 2.

"On Some Criticisms of Whitehead's Philosophy", *Philosophical Review*, XLIV, 4 (July, 1935), 323 – 344.

"Ontological Primacy; a Reply to Buchler", *Journal of Philosophy*, LXXVII, 23 (Dec. 10, 1970), 979 – 986.

"Order and Chaos", *The Concept of Order*, ed. Paul G. Kuntz. Seattle: University of Washington Press, 1968, 253 – 267.

"The Organism according to Process Philosophy", *Organism, Medicine, and Metaphysics: Essays in Honor of Hans Jonas on his 75th Birthday*, ed. Stuart F. Dordrecht Spicker. Holland: D. Reidel, 1978, 137 – 154.

"Outlines of a Philosophy of Nature, Part I", *Personalist*, XXXIX, 3 (Summer, July, 1958), 239 – 248; "Part II", *Ibid.*, XXXIX, 4 (Autumn, Oct., 1958), 380 – 391.

"Pansychism", *A History of Philosophical Systems*, ed. Vergilius Ferm. N.Y.: Philosophical Library, 1950, 442 – 453.

"Pansychism: Mind as Sole Reality", *Ultimate Reality and Meaning*, I, 2, (1978), 115 – 129.

"Pantheism", *Encyclopedia Britannica* (1967, Vol. 17), 233 – 234.

"Paul Weiss's *The God We Seek*", *Review of Metaphysics*, XXV, Suppl. (June, 1972), 108 – 116.

"Pepper's Approach to Metaphysics", *Root Metaphor: The Live Thought of Stephen C. Pepper*: PAUNCH 53 – 54 (1980), 80 – 81.

"Perception and the Concrete Abstractness of Science", *Philosophy and Phenomenological Research*, XXXIV, 4 (June, 1974), 465 – 476.

"Personal Identity from A to Z", *Process Studies*, II, 3 (Fall, 1972), 209 – 215.

"A Philosopher's Assessment of Christianity", *Religion and Culture: Essays in Honor of Paul Tillich*, ed. Walter Leibrecht. N.Y.: Harper, 1959, 167 – 180.

"The Philosophical Limitations of Humanism", *University Review*, III, 4 (Summer, 1937), 240 – 242.

"Philosophy After Fifty Years", *Mid-Twentieth Century American Philosophy: Personal Statements*, ed. Peter A. Bertocci. N.Y.: Humanities Press, 1974, 140 – 154.

"Philosophy and Orthodoxy", *Ethics*, LIV, 4 (July, 1944), 295 – 298.

"The Philosophy of Creative Synthesis", Symposium: Creativity as a Philosophical Category, *Journal of Philosophy*, LV, 22 (Oct. 23, 1958), 944 – 953.

"A Philosophy of Death", *Philosophical Aspects of Thanatology*, Vol. II, eds. Florence M. Hetzler and A.H. Kutscher. N.Y.: MSS Information Corporation, 1978, 81 – 89.

"Physics and Psychics: The Place of Mind in Nature", *Mind in Nature: Essays on the Interface of Science and Philosophy* Washington, D.C.: University Press of America, 1977. 89 – 96.

"Politics and the Metaphysics of Freedom", *Enquête sur la liberté, Fédération internationale des sociétés de philosophie.* Publié avec le concours de l'UNESCO Paris: Hermann, 1953, 79 – 85.

"Present Prospects for Metaphysics", *Monist*, XLVII, 2 (Winter, 1963), 188 – 210.

"The Principle of Shared Creativity", *Unitarian Symposia No. 6 What Can Religion Offer Modern Man?*, April, 1959, 1 – 8.

"Process Philosophy as a Resource for Christian Thought", *Philosophical Resources for Christian Thought*, ed. Perry LeFevre. Nashville: Abingdon, 1968, 44 – 66.

"Process and the Nature of God", *Traces of God in a Secular Culture*, ed. George F. McLean. N.Y.: Alba House, 1973, 117 – 141.

"Process as Inclusive Category: a Reply to John E. Smith", *Journal of Philosophy*, LII, 4 (Feb. 17, 1955), 94 – 102.

"Process Themes in Chinese Thought", *Journal of Chinese Philosophy*, VI (1979), 323 – 336.

"Psychicalism and the Leibnizian Principle", *Studia Leibnitiana*, VIII, 2 (1976), 154 – 159.

"Psychology and the Unity of Knowledge", *Southern Journal of Philosophy*, V, 2 (Summer, 1967), 81 – 90.

"Radhakrishnan on Mind, Matter, and God", *The Philosophy of Sarvepalli Radhakrishnan*, ed. Paul Arthur Schilpp. The Library of Living Philosophers, Vol. VIII. N.Y.: Tudor, 1952, 313 – 322.

"Rationale of the Ontological Proof", *Theology Today*, XX, 2 (July, 1963), 278 – 283.

"The Rationalistic Criterion in Metaphysics", *Philosophy and Phenomenological Research*, VIII, 3 (March, 1948), 436 – 447.

"Real Possibility", *Journal of Philosophy*, LX, 21 (Oct. 10, 1963), 593 – 605.

"The Reality of the Past, the Unreality of the Future", *Hibbert Journal*, XXXVII, 2 (Jan., 1939), 246 – 257.

"Rechte – nicht nur für die Menschen", tr. Dr Ilse Tödt, *Zeitschrift für Evangelische Ethik*, XXII, 1 (Jan., 1978), 3 – 14.

"Redefining God", *New Humanist*, VII, 4 (July – Aug., 1934), 8 – 15.

"Reflections on the Strength and Weakness of Thomism", *Ethics*, LIV, 1 (Oct., 1943), 53 – 57.

"Relative, Absolute, and Superrelative: a Formal Analysis", *Philosophical Review*, LV, 3 (May, 1946), 213 – 228.

136

"The Relativity of Nonrelativity: Some Reflections on Firstness". *Studies in the Philosophy of Charles Sanders Peirce*, eds. Philipp P. Wiener and Frederic H. Young. Cambridge: Harvard University Press, 1952, 215 – 224.

"Religion and Creative Experience", *Darshana, an International Quarterly of Philosophy, Psychology, Psychical Research, Religion, Mysticism and Sociology* (India), II, 1 (Jan., 1962) 47 – 52.

"Religion and Creative Experience", *Unitarian Register and Univeralist Leader*, CXLI, 6 (June, 1962), 9 – 11.

"Religion in Process Philosophy", *Religion in Philosophical and Cultural Perspective*, eds. J. Clayton Feaver and William Horosz. Princeton: D. van Nostrand, 1967, 246 – 268.

"Religious Aspects of Necessity and Contingency", *Great Issues Concerning Theism*, ed. Charles H. Monson, Jr. Salt Lake City: University of Utah Press, 1965, 147 – 164.

"Reply to Father Meehan", *Journal of Religion*, XXVI, 1 (Jan., 1946), 54 – 57.

"The Rights of the Subhuman World", *Environmental Ethics: an Interdisciplinary Journal Dedicated to the Philosophical Aspects of Environmental Problems*, I, 1 (Spring, 1979), 49 – 60.

"Royce and the Collapse of Idealism", *Revue internationale de philosophie*, XXIII, 79 – 80 (1967, Fasc. 1 – 2), 46 – 59.

"The Significance of Man in the Life of God", *Theology in Crisis: a Colloquium on "The Credibility of God"*. New Concord, Ohio: Muskingum College, 1967, 40 – 43.

"Six Theistic Proofs", *Monist*, LIV, 2 (April, 1970), 159 – 180.

"The Social Structure of Experience", *Philosophy*, XXXVI, 137 (April and July, 1961), 97 – 111.

"The Social Theory of Feelings", *Persons, Privacy, and Feeling: Essays in the Philosophy of Mind*, ed. Dwight Van de Vate, Jr. Memphis: Memphis State University Press, 1970, 39 – 51.

"Some Empty though Important Truths", *Review of Metaphysics,* VIII, 4 (June, 1955), 553 – 568. Reprinted in *American Philosophers at Work: the Philosophic Scene in the United States*, ed. Sidney Hook. N.Y.: Criterion Books, 1956, 225 – 235.

"Some Reflections on Metaphysics and Language", *Foundations of Language: International Journal of Language and Philosophy,* II, 1 (Feb., 1966), 20 – 32.

"Some Thoughts on "Souls" and Neighborly Love", *Anglican Theological Review*, LV, 2 (April, 1973), 144 – 147.

"Spirit as Life Freely Participating in Life", *Biosophical Review*, X, 2 (1953), 31 – 32.

"Strict and Genetic Identity: an Illustration of the Relations of Logic to Metaphysics", *Structure, Method, and Meaning: Essays in Honor of Henry M. Sheffer*, ed. Horace M. Kallen et al. N.Y.: Liberal Arts Press, 1951, 242 – 254.

"The Structure of Givenness", *Philosophical forum*, XVIII (1960 – 61), 22 – 39.

"The Structure of Metaphysics: a Criticism of Lazerowitz's Theory", *Philosophy and Phenomenological Research*, XIX, 2 (Dec., 1958), 226 – 240.

"Synthesis as Polyadic Inclusion: a Reply to Sessions", *Southern Journal of Philosophy*, XIV (Summer, 1976), 245 – 255.

"The Synthesis of Idealism and Realism", *Theoria* (Sweden) XV, (March 12, 1949), 90 – 107.

"Theism in Asian and Western Thought", *Philosophy East and West*, XXVIII, 4 (Oct., 1978), 401 – 411.

"The Theistic Proofs", *Union Seminary Quarterly Review*, XX, 2 (Jan., 1965), 115 – 129.

"Theological Values in Current Metaphysics", *Journal of Religion*, XX, 3 (July, 1946), 157 – 167.

"The Three Ideas of God", *Journal of Liberal Religion*, I, 3 (Winter, 1940), 9 – 16.

"Tillich and the Other Great Tradition", *Anglican Theological Review*, XLIII, 3 (July, 1961), 245 – 259.

"Tillich and the Non-theological Meaning of Theological Terms", *Religion in Life*, XXXV, 5 (Winter, 1966), 674 – 685. Reprinted in *Paul Tillich: Retrospect and Future*. Nashville: Abingdon Press, 1966, 19 – 30.

"Tillich's Doctrine of God", *The Theology of Paul Tillich*. The Library of Living Theology, Vol. 1, eds. Charles W. Kegley and Robert W. Bretall. N.Y.: Macmillan, 1952, 164 – 195.

"Tragic and Sublime Aspects of Christian Love", *Journal of Liberal Religion*, VIII, 1 (Summer, 1946), 36 – 44.

"Twelve Elements of My Philosophy", *The Southwestern Journal of Philosophy*, V, 1 (Spring, 1974), 7 – 15.

"Two Forms of Idolatry", *International Journal for Philosophy of Religion*, I, 1 (Spring, 1970), 3 – 15.

"Two Levels of Faith and Reason", *Journal of Bible and Religion*, XVI, 1 (Jan., 1948), 30 – 38.

"The Two Possible Philosophical Definitions of God", *Actas: XIII Congreso International de Filosofía*. Mexico City: Universidad Nacional Autonoma de Mexico, 1966, Vol. IX, 121.

"Two Strata of Meaning in Religious Discourse", Symposium on Philosophy of Religion, *Southern Philosopher*, V, 3 (Oct. 1956), 4 – 7.

"The Unity of Man and the Unity of Nature", *Emory University Quarterly*, XI, 3 (Oct., 1955), 129 – 141.

"What Did Anselm Discover?", *The Many-Faced Argument*, eds. John Hick and Arthur C. McGill. N.Y.: Macmillan, 1967, 321 – 333.

"What Metaphysics Is", *Journal of Karnatak University: Social Sciences*, III, 1967, 1 – 15.

"What the Ontological Proof Does not Do", *Review of Metaphysics*, XVII, 4 (June, 1964), 608 – 609.

"Whitehead and Berdyaev: Is There Tragedy in God?", *Journal of Religion*, XXXVII, 2 (April, 1957), 71 – 84.

"Whitehead and Leibniz: a Comparison", *Contemporary Studies in Philosophical Idealism*, eds. John Howie and Thomas O. Buford. Cape Cod, Mass.: Claude Starke and Company, 1975, 95 – 115.

"Whitehead and Ordinary Language", *Southern Journal of Philosophy*, VII, 4 (Winter, 1969 – 1970), 437 – 445.

"Whitehead in French Perspective", *Thomist*, XXXIII, 3 (July 1969), 573 – 381.

"Whitehead on Process: a Reply to Professor Eslick", *Philosophy and Phenomenological Research*, XVIII, 4 (June, 1958), 514 – 520.

"Whitehead's Conception of God" and "Whitehead's Theory of Prehension", *Actas: Segundo Congreso Extraordinario Inter-americano de Filosofia*, 22 – 26 Julio, 1961. San Jose, Costa Rica: Imprenta Nacional, 1963, 163 – 170.

"Whitehead's Differences from Buddhism", *Philosophy East and West*, XXV, 4 (Oct., 1975), 407 – 413.

"Whitehaed's Idea of God", *The Philosophy of Alfred North Whitehead*, ed. Paul Arthur Schilpp. The Library of Living Philosophers. Vol. III. Evanston and Chicago: Northwestern University, 1941, 513 – 559.

"Whitehead's Novel Intuition", *Alfred North Whitehead: Essays on His Philosophy*, ed. George L. Kline. Englewood Cliffs, N.J.: Prentice-Hall, 1963, 18 – 26.

"Whitehead's Philosophy of Reality as Socially-Structured Process", (apropros *Alfred North Whitehead: An Anthology* selected by F.S.C. Northrop and Mason Gross), *Chicago Review*, VIII, 2 (Spring – Summer, 1954), 60 – 77.

"Whitehead's Revolutionary Concept of Prehension", *International Philosophical Quarterly*, XIX, 3 (Sept., 1979), 253 – 263.

"Why Psychicalism? Comments on Keeling's and Shepherd's Criticisms", *Process Studies*, VI, 1 (Spring, 1976), 67 – 72.

SECONDARY SOURCES

Bertocci, Peter A. "Hartshorne on Personal Identity", *Process Studies*, II (1972), 216 – 221.

Birch, Charles. "What Does God Do in the World?", *Union Seminary Quarterly Review*, XXX, 2 – 4 (Winter – Summer, 1975), 76 – 84.

Blaitry, Tobias Diaz. *La Idea de Dios en Charles Hartshorne*. Universidad de Panama, 1967.

Blaikie, R.J. "Being, Process, and Action in Modern Philosophy and Theology", *Scotish Journal of Theology*, XXV (May, 1972).

Brown, Delwin. "Recent Process Theology", *Journal of the American Academy of Religion*, XXXV, 1 (March 1967), 28 – 41.

Brown, Delwin, Ralph E. James, Jr. and Gene Reeves, eds. *Process Philosophy and Christian Thought*. Indianapolis: Bobbs-Merrill, 1971.

Browning, Douglas, ed. *Philosophers of Process*. N.Y.: Random House, 1965.

Burkle, H.R. "God's Relation to the World: The Issues between St. Thomas Aquinas and Charles Hartshorne." Dissertation, Yale University, 1964.

Burkle, H.R. *The Non-Existence of God*. N.Y.: Herder and Herder, 1969.

Burrell, David B. *Aquinas: God and Action*. Notre Dame: University of Notre Dame Press, 1979.

Cahn, Steven M. *Fate, Logic and Time*. Yale University Press, 1967.

Cahn, Steven M. "Review of NTOT", *Journal of Philosophy*, LXV, 8 (April 18, 1968).

Capek, Milic. *The Philosophical Impact of Contemporary Physics*. Princeton: D. van Nostrand Co., 1962.

Cargas, Henry James and Bernard Lee, eds. *Religious Experience and Process Theology*. N.Y.: Paulist Press, 1976.

Clarke, W. Norris. *The Philosophical Approach to God: A Neo-Thomistic Perspective*. Winston-Salem, N.C.: Wake Forest University, 1979.

Cobb, John B. Jr. *A Christian Natural Theology Based on the Thought of A.N. Whitehead*. Philadelphia: Westminster Press, 1965.

Cobb, John B. Jr. "Perfection Exists: a Critique of Charles Hartshorne", *Religion in Life* (Spring, 1963), 294 – 304.

Cobb, John B. Jr. *Process Theology as Political Theology* Manchester University Press/Westminster Press, 1982.

Cobb, John B. Jr. "Speaking About God", *Religion in Life*, XXXVI 1 (1967), 28 – 39.

Cobb, John B. Jr. and David R. Griffin. *Process Theology: an Introductory Exposition*. Belfast: Christian Journals, 1976.

Cousins, Ewert H., ed. *Process Theology: Basic Writings*. N.Y.: Newman Press, 1971.

Craighead, Houston. "Non-Being and Hartshorne's Concept of God", *Process Studies*, I (1971), 9 – 24.

Davies, Brian, "God, Time and Change", *Clergy Review* (February, 1978), 68 – 72.

Davis, Stephen, ed. *Encountering Evil: Live Options in Theodicy*. T & T Clark, 1981.

Dean, William. "An American Theology", *Process Studies*, XII, 2 (Summer, 1982), 111 – 128.

Donceel, Joseph. "Second Thoughts on the Nature of God", *Thought*, XLVI, 182 (1971), 346 – 370.

Etzwiler, James P. "Being as Activity in Aristotle: a Process Interpretation", *International Philosophical Quarterly*, XVIII, 3 (Sept., 1978), 311 – 334.

Evans, D. Luther. "Two Intellectually Respectable Conceptions of God", *Philosophy and Phenomenological Research*, X (1950), 572 – 577.

Feaver, J. Clayton and William Horosz, eds. *Religion in Philosophical and Cultural Perspective*. Princeton: D. van Nostrand Co., 1967.

Felt, James W. "Invitation to a Philosophic Revolution", *The New Scholasticism*, XLV, 1 (Winter, 1971), 87 – 109.

Ferm, Vergilius, ed. *A History of Philosophical Systems*. N.Y.: Philosophical Library, 1950.

Ferre, Nels F.S. "Beyond Substance and Process", *Theology Today*, XXIV (1967), 160 – 171.

Fitzgerald, Paul. "Relativity Physics and the God of Process Philosophy", *Process Studies*, II, 4 (Winter, 1972), 251 – 73.

Ford, Lewis S. "Divine Persuasion and the Triumph of the God", *Christian Scholar*, L. 3 (Fall, 1967).

Ford, Lewis S. "God as King: Benevolent Despot or Constitutional Monarch?", *Christian Scholar's Review*, I, 4 (1971), 318 – 322.

Ford, Lewis S. "Is Process Theism Compatible with Relativity Theory?", *Journal of Religion*, XLVIII, 2 (April, 1968), 124 – 135.

Ford, Lewis S., ed. *Two Process Philosophers: Hartshorne's Encounter with Whitehead*. AAR Studies in Religion, No. 5. Tallahasse, Florida: American Academy of Religion, 1973.

Forsyth, T.M. "Creative Evolution in Its Bearing on the Idea of God", *Philosophy*, XXV, 94 (July, 1950), 195 – 208.

Fost, F.F. "The Philosophical Theology of Charles Hartshorne: an Analysis and Critique of the Categories of Dipolar Theism." Dissertation, Claremont Graduate School, 1964.

Garland, William J. "The Ultimacy of Creativity", *Southern Journal of Philosophy*, (Winter, 1969), 361 – 376.

Gibson, A. Boyce. "Empirical Evidence and Religious Faith", *Journal of Religion*, XXXV (1956), 24 – 35.

Gibson, A. Boyce. *Theism and Empiricism*. SCM Press, 1970.

Gill, Jerry H., ed. *Philosophy and Religion: Some Contemporary Perspectives*. Mineapolis: Burgess, 1968.

Gragg, Alan. *Charles Hartshorne*. Waco, Texas: Word Books, Publishers, 1973.

Griffin, David R. "Actuality, Possibility and Theodicy", *Process Studies* (Fall, 1982).

Griffin, David R. *God, Power and Evil: a Process Theodicy*. Philadelphia: The Westminster Press, 1976.

Gunton, Colin E. *Becoming and Being: The Doctrine of God in Charles Hartshorne and Karl Barth*. Oxford University Press, 1978.

Gunton, Colin E. "The Knowledge of God According to Two Process Theologians: a Twentieth-Century Gnosticism", *Religious Studies*, XI, 1 (March, 1975), 87 – 96.

Gunton, Colin E. "Process Theology's Concept of God: an Outline and Assessment", *The Expository Times*, LXXXIV (1972 – 73), 292 – 296.

Gunton, Colin E. "Rejection, Influence and Development: Hartshorne in the History of Philosophy", *Process Studies*, VI, 1 (Spring, 1976), 33 – 42.

Hartt, Julian. "The Logic of Perfection", *Review of Metaphysics*, XVI, 4 (June, 1963), 749 – 769.

Hachett, Marion J. "Charles Hartshorne's Critique of Christian Theology", *Anglican Theological Review*, XLVIII (1966), 264 – 275.

Haught, John F. "Dipolar Theism: Psychological Considerations", *Process Studies*, VI, 1 (Spring, 1976), 45 – 50.

Henry, Carl F.H. "The Reality and Identity of God: Part I", *Christianity Today*, XIII, 12 (March 14, 1969), 523 – 526. "Part II", *Ibid.*, XIII, 13 (March 28, 1969), 580 – 584.

Henry, Jerry Clay, "Immortality in the Thought of Charles Hartshorne", Ph.D. Dissertation, Baylor University, 1975.

Hocking, Richard. "Event, Act, and Presence", *Review of Metaphysics*, XXIV, 1 (1970).

Hook, Sidney, ed. *Religious Experience and Truth*. N.Y.: New York University Press, 1961.

Janzen, J. Gerald. "Modes of Power and the Divine Relativity", *Encounter*, XXXVI, 4 (Autumn, 1975), 379 – 406.

Johnson, Galen A. "Hartshorne's Arguments Against Empirical Evidence for Necessary Existence: an Evaluation". *Religious Studies*, XIII, 175 – 187.
Keeling, L. Bryant. "Feeling as a Metaphysical Category: Hartshorne from an Analytical View". *Process Studies*, VI, 1 (Spring, 1976), 51 – 66.
Kelly, Geffrey B. "The Nature of God in Process Theology", *Irish Theological Quarterly*, XVI, 1 (1979), 1 – 20.
King, J. Norman and Barry L. Whitney. "Rahner and Hartshorne on Divine Immutability", *International Philosophical Quarterly*, XXII, 3 (Sept., 1982), 195 – 209.
Klibansky, Raymond, ed. *Contemporary Philosophy; a Survey*. Florence: La Nuova Italia Editrice, 1969.
Knasas, John F.X. "Aquinas and Finite Gods", *Proceedings of the American Catholic Philosophical Association*, LIII (1979), 88 – 97.
Kuntz, Paul G., ed. *The Concept of Order*. Seattle: University of Washington Press, 1968.
Lachs, John. "Two Concepts of God", *Harvard Theological Review*, LIX, 3 (1966), 227 – 240.
Le Fevre, Perry, ed. *Philosophical Resources for Christian Thought*. Nashville: Abingdon Press, 1968.
Lieb, Irwin C., ed. *Experience, Existence and the Good: Essays in Honor of Paul Weiss*. Carbondale: Southern Illinois University Press, 1961.
Loomer, Bernard. "Two Conceptions of Power", *Process Studies*, VI, 1 (Spring, 1976), 5 – 32.
Lucas, George R., Jr. *The Genesis of Modern Process Thought: A Historical Outline with Bibliography*. Metuchen, N.J. and London: Scarecrow Press, 1983.
Lycan, W. Gregory. "Hartshorne and Findlay on "Necessity" in the Ontological Argument", *Philosophical Studies*, XVII (1968), 132 – 141.
McLean, George F., ed. *Traces of God in a Secular Culture*. 2 Vols. N.Y.: Alba House, 1973.
Martin, R.M. "On Hartshorne's "Creative Synthesis" and Event Logic", *Southern Journal of Philosophy*, IX, 4 (Winter, 1971), 399 – 410.
Mascall, E.L. *The Openness of Being*. London: Darton, Longman & Todd, 1971.
Mason, David. "An Examination of "Worship" as a Key for Re-examining the God-Problem", *Journal of Religion*, LV, (1975), 76 – 94.
Matczak, S.A., ed. *God in Contemporary Thought*. N.Y.: Learned Publications, 1977.
Meland, Bernard E., ed. *The Future of Empirical Theology*. Chicago: The University of Chicago Press, 1969.

Meynell, Hugo. "The Theology of Hartshorne", *Journal of Theological Studies*, N.S. XXIV, 1 (April, 1973), 143 – 157.

Minor, William S., ed. *Directives from Charles Hartshorne and Henry Nelson Wieman Critically Analyzed.* Philosophy of Creativity Monograph Series, Vol. I. Carbondale: The Foundation for Creative Philosophy, Inc., 1969.

Nelson, Herbert J. "The Epistemic Availability of Hartshorne's "Experience": a Critical Analysis", *International Philosophical Quarterly*, XXI, 1 (March, 1981), 29 – 49.

Nelson, Herbert. "The Resting Place of Process Theology", *Harvard Theological Review*, LXXII, 1 – 2 (Jan. – April, 1979), 1 – 21.

Neville, Robert. *Creativity and God: a Challenge to Process Theology.* Seabury Press, 1980.

Neville, Robert. "Experience and Philosophy: a Review of Hartshorne's CSPM", *Process Studies*, II (1972), 49 – 67.

Neville, Robert. *God the Creator: on the Transcendence and Presence of God.* Chicago: The University of Chicago Press, 1968.

Neville, Robert. "Neoclassical Metaphysics and Christianity", *International Philosophical Quarterly*, X (1969), 605 – 624.

Oakes, Robert A. "Classical Theism and Pantheism: a Victory for Process Theism?", *Religious Studies,* XIII, 167 – 173.

O'Donnell, John. *Trinity and Temporality: The Christian Doctrine of God in the Light of Process Theology and the Theology of Hope.* Oxford University Press, 1983.

Ogden, Schubert M. "Faith and Truth", *Christian Century*, LXXXII, 32 (Sept. 1, 1965), 1057 – 1060.

Ogden, Schubert M. "God and Philosophy: a Discussion with Anthony Flew", *Journal of Religion*, XLVIII, 2 (April, 1968), 161 – 181.

Ogden, Schubert. "The Possibility and Task of Philosophical Theology", *Union Seminary Quarterly*, XX (1965).

Ogden, Schubert. *The Reality of God and Other Essays.* N.Y.: Harper & Row, 1966.

Ogden, Schubert. "Theology and Metaphysics", *Criterion*, IX (Autumn, 1969), 15 – 18.

Ogden, Schubert. "Theology and Philosophy: a New Phase of the Discussion", *The Journal of Religion*, XLIV, 1 (January, 1964), 1 – 16.

Ogletree, Thomas W. "A Christological Assessment of Dipolar Theism". *The Journal of Religion*, XLVII, 2 (April, 1967), 87 – 99.

Owen, H.P. *Concepts of Deity.* London: Macmillan, 1971.

Pailin, David. "Neville's Critique of Hartshorne", *Process Studies*, IV (Fall, 1974), 187 – 198.

Pailin, David. "Process Theology – Why and What?" *Faith and Thought*, C, 1 (1972), 45 – 66.

Pailin, David. "Some Comments on Hartshorne's Presentation of the Ontological Argument", *Religious Studies*, IV (1968), 103 – 122.

Palmer, Michael F. "Hartshorne's Critique of Tillich's Theory of Religious Symbolism". *Heythrop Journal*, XVII, 4 (1976), 379 – 394.

Parker, Francis H. "Head, Heart, and God". *Review of Metaphysics*, XIV, 2 (Dec., 1960), 328 – 352.

Peden, Creighton. *Wieman's Empirical Process Philosophy*. Washington, D.C.: University Press of America, 1977.

Peters, Eugene H. *The Creative Advance: An Introduction to Process Philosophy as a Context for Christian Faith*. The Library of Contemporary Theology. St. Louis: The Bethany Press, 1966.

Peters, Eugene H. "A Framework for Christian Thought", *Journal of Religion*, XLVI (July, 1966), 374 – 385.

Peters, Eugene H. "Hartshorne on Actuality", *Process Studies*, VII, 3 (Fall, 1977), 200 – 204.

Peters, Eugene H. *Hartshorne and Neoclassical Metaphysics: an Interpretation*. Lincoln: University of Nebraska Press, 1970.

Peters, Eugene. "Philosophic Insights of Charles Hartshorne", *The Southwestern Journal of Philosophy*, VIII, 1 (Winter, 1977), 157 – 170.

Pike, Nelson. *God and Timelessness*. London: Routledge & Kegan Paul, 1970.

Pike, Nelson, "Process Theodicy and the Concept of Power", *Process Studies* (Fall, 1982).

Pittenger, Norman. *Catholic Faith in a Process Perspective*. Orbis Books, 1981.

Pittenger, Norman. *God in Process*. London: SCM Press, 1967.

Pittenger, Norman. *Picturing God*. SCM Press, 1982.

Pittenger, Norman. "Towards an Understanding of the Self". in *Contemporary Studies in Philosophical Idealism* (Bertocci Festschrift), eds. John Howie and Thomas O. Buford. Cape Cod: Claude Stark & Co., 1975, 161 – 172.

Power, William L. "Descriptive Language and the Term "God"". *International Journal for Philosophy of Religion*, III, 4 (1972), 223 – 239.

Rattigan, Mary T. "The Concept of God in Process Thought", *Irish Theological Quarterly*, XLIX, 3 (1982), 206 – 215.

Reck, Andrew J. "The Philosophy of Charles Hartshorne", *Studies in Whitehead's Philosophy*. Tulane Studies in Philosophy, Vol. X (1961), 89 – 108.

Reese, William L. and Eugene Freeman, eds. *Process and Divinity: The Hartshorne 'Festschrift': Philosophical Essays Presented to Charles Hartshorne*. La Salle: Open Court, 1964.

Reeves, Gene. "God and Creativity", *Southern Journal of Philosophy*, (Winter, 1969), 377 – 385.

Reitz, H. "Was ist Prozesstheologie? Analyse eines Neuansatzes in der nordamerikanischen Theologie der Gegenwart", *Kerygma und Dogma*, XVI, 2 (1970), 78 – 103.

Richardson, David B. "Philosophies of Hartshorne and Teilhard de Chardin: Two Sides of the Same Coin?", *Southern Journal of Philosophy*, II, 3 (Fall, 1964), 107 – 115.

Richardson, Herbert W. and Donal R. Cutler, eds. *Transcendence*. Boston: Beacon Press, 1969.

Robertson, John C. Jr. "Does God Change?", *Ecumenist*, IX 4 (1971), 61 – 64.

Rome, Beatrice K. and Sydney C., eds. *Philosophical Interrogations*. N.Y.: Holt, Rinehart and Winston, 1964.

Ruf, Henry L. "The Impossibility of Hartshorne's God", *Philosophical Forum*, VII, 3 – 4 (Spring – Summer, 1976), 345 – 363.

Schedler, Norbert O. *Philosophy of Religion: Contemporary Perspectives*. N.Y.: Macmillan, 1974.

Schindler, David L. "Whitehead's Challenge to Thomism on the Problem of God: The Metaphysical Issues", *International Philosophical Quarterly*, XIX, 3 Issue No. 75 (Sept., 1979), 285 – 299.

Schoonenberg, Piet. "God as Relating and (Be)Coming: A Meta-Thomistic Consideration", *Listening*, XIV, 3 (Fall, 1979), 265 – 280.

Schoonenberg, Piet. "Process or History in God?" *Louvain Studies*, IV, 4 (1973), 303 – 319.

Schurr, V., "Was ist Prozesstheologie?", *Theologie der Gegenwart*, XIII (1970), 181 – 183.

Sessions, William Lad, "Charles Hartshorne and Thirdness", *Southern Journal of Philosophy*, XII (1974), 239.

Sessions, William Lad. "A Critical Examination of Dipolar Panentheism." Dissertation, Yale University, 1971.

Shalom, Albert and John C. Robertson, Jr. "Hartshorne and the Problem of Personal Identity", *Process Studies*, VIII, 3 (Fall, 1978), 169 – 179.

Sia, Santiago. "On God, Time and Change", *Clergy Review,* LXIII, 10 (October, 1978), 378 – 387.

Sia, Santiago. "An Interview with Charles Hartshorne", *Milltown Studies*, No. 4 (Autumn, 1979), 1 – 23.

Sibley, Jack R. and Pete A.Y. Gunter, eds. *Process Philosophy: Basic*

Writings. Washington: University Press of America, 1978.

Smith, John E., ed. *Contemporary American Philosophy: Second Series.* London: Allen and Unwin, 1970.

Sontag, Frederick. "Hartshorne as Idealist", *Journal of Religion*, LIII, 2 (1973), 247 – 250.

Spiceland, James D. "Process Theology", in *One God in Trinity*, eds. Peter Toon and James D. Spiceland. Westchester, Ill.: Cornerston Books, 1980, 133 – 157.

Stearns, J. Brenton. "Becoming: a Problem for Determinists?", *Process Studies*, VI, 4 (Winter, 1976), 237 – 248.

Stokes, Walter E. "Is God Really Related to the World?", *Proceedings of the American Catholic Philosophical Association*. Washington: CUA, 1965.

Thomason, Sister Adelaide. "An Examination and Application of the Law of Contrast in Charles Hartshorne's Panentheism." Dissertation, Fordham University, 1969.

Towne, Edgard A. "Metaphysics as Method in Charles Hartshorne's Thought", *Southern Journal of Philosophy*, VI, 3 (Fall, 1968), 125 – 142.

Tracy, David. *Blassed Rage for Order: The New Pluralism in Theology.* N.Y.: Seabury Press, 1975.

Trethowan, Illtyd. "God's Changelessness", *Clergy Review* (January, 1979), 15 – 21.

Van der Veken, J. "Dieu et la Réalité: Introduction à la "Process Theology"", *Revue Theologique de Louvain*, IV (1977), 423 – 447.

Van der Veken, J. "Toward a Dipolar View on the Whole of Reality", trans. from the Dutch by Hans Kothius. *Louvain Studies*, VII, 2 (Fall, 1978), 102 – 114.

Vaught, C.G. "Contemporary Conceptions of the Nature and Existence of God: a Study of Tillich and Hartshorne". Dissertation, Yale University, 1966.

Vaught, C.G. "Hartshorne's Ontological Argument: an Instance of Misplaced Concreteness", *International Journal for Philosophy of Religion*, III, 1 (1972), 18 – 34.

Vieth, R.F. "The Logic of Religion in the Philosophy of Charles Hartshorne." Dissertation, Southern Methodist University, 1972.

Westphal, Merold. "Temporality and Finitism in Hartshorne's Theism". *Review of Metaphysics*, XIX (1965 – 66), 550 – 564.

Whitehead, A.N. *Adventures of Ideas.* London: Cambridge University Press, 1933.

Whitehead, A.N. *Modes of Thought.* London: Cambridge University Press, 1938.

Whitehead, A.N. *Process and Reality.* corrected ed. Edited by David Ray Griffin and Donald Sherburne. N.Y.: Free Press, 1978.

Whitehead, A.N. *Religion in the Making.* London: Cambridge University Press, 1926.

Whitehead, A.N. *Science and the Modern World.* London: Cambridge University Press, 1936.

Whitney, Barry L. "Divine Immutability in Process Philosophy and Contemporary Thomism", *Horizons*, VII (1980), 49 – 68.

Whitney, Barry L. "Hartshorne's New Look at Theodicy", *Studies in Religion*, VIII (1979), 281 – 291.

Whitney, Barry L. "Process Theism: Does a Persuasive God Coerce?", *The Southern Journal of Philosophy*, XVII, 1 (1979), 138 – 143.

Wilcox, John T. "Hartshorne's Indeterminism: a Preliminary Appraisal", *Philosophy Today*, XXI, 1 (Spring, 1977), 62 – 73.

Wilcox, John T. "A Question from Physics for Certain Theists", *Journal of Religion*, XLI, 4 (October, 1961), 293 – 300.

Wild, John. "The Divine Existence: an Answer to Mr. Hartshorne", *Review of Metaphysics*, IV, 1 (Sept., 1950), 61 – 84.

Wild, John. "A Review-Article: Hartshorne's DR", *Review of Metaphysics*, II, 6 (1948), 65 – 77.

Wild, Robert. *Who I Will Be: Is There Joy and Sorrow in God?* Denville, N.J.: Dimension Books, 1976.

Wright, John H. "Divine Knowledge and Human Freedom: The God who Dialogues", *Theological Studies*, XXXVIII, 3 (Sept., 1977), 450 – 477.

Wiltshire, Susan Ford. "Process Theology and God as Parent", *The Christian Century*, XCIV, 31 (Oct. 5, 1977), 874 – 876.

INDEX

150

152